Living Full-Tilt

Proven Principles for Living Your Life in Freedom, Joy and Plenty

Janie Kelley

BALBOA
PRESS
A DIVISION OF HAY HOUSE

Balboa Press books may be ordered through booksellers or by contacting:

Balboa Press
A Division of Hay House
1663 Liberty Drive
Bloomington, IN 47403
www.balboapress.com
1 (877) 407-4847

Print information available on the last page.

ISBN: 978-1-5043-7736-2 (sc)
ISBN: 978-1-5043-7738-6 (hc)
ISBN: 978-1-5043-7737-9 (e)

Library of Congress Control Number: 2017904341

Balboa Press rev. date: 05/05/2017

Dedication

To my brave and beautiful sister

Susie

TABLE OF CONTENTS

Acknowledgments

I feel a deep sense of gratitude to all those who have helped me learn and grow. There is a special place in my heart for those beautiful souls who have encouraged me during the writing of this book. My gratitude extends to Lynn and Dee Averyt, Sandy Barth, Rose Marie Benisek, Becky Benes, Edwene Gaines, Jeff Greenwood, Jane Johnson, Rashda Kahn, Bob and Jannette Kavisic, Louise Korona, Jan Lancaster, Becky Martin, Deborah Michalewicz, Barbara Mobley, Terry and Diane Mobley, Gloria Neumeyer, Mejo Okon, Valerie Queen, Ara Rahman, Bill Reynolds, Dott Richardel, Teresa Rylander, Linda Sawyer, Louis Shosty, Catherine Taylor, Jim and Mary Tufts, Paula Walker, John Welty, Toolie Wiedenhofer, The Abundance Angels and the loving and supportive people of Unity Spiritual Center-San Angelo.

Special thanks to Catherine Taylor and L. Joseph Shosty for editing this book.

I send deep appreciation to my sisters Evelyn and Linda and to my supportive family.

I offer profound, open-hearted gratitude to Keith Kelley, Honey Velleca, and Kevin Kelley for being my sons, my daughter and my teachers of unconditional love and forgiveness.

I give my most immeasurable gratitude to my, patient, kind and loving husband, Danny.

I would be remiss if I did not mention my loving canine family, Freckles and BoBo, who remind me daily of who I really am.

FOREWORD

Wayne Dyer wrote, "When you change the way you look at things, the things you look at change."

Author, Janie Kelley, offers us powerful tools, technics and instructions for making simple, yet life altering, changes. These simple changes will empower us to live *Full-Tilt*.

The world is ready for this life changing information which shows how to change our minds and change our behaviors. This, then, allows us to release the past, the old ideas, habits and behaviors which no longer serve us but keep us stuck in ruts. These ruts take us nowhere new, fresh and exciting.

This delightful guide to self-empowerment gives us intelligent reminders of our own worthiness and deservability of good and of all good.

Each of us, she reminds us, must focus a part of our life experience on solitude in order to listen and understand. Her deep insights into our own longing to live an abundant, joy-filled life lead us to embrace the helpful meditation practices that she provides.

This book shows us clearly the power of money in our lives. It reminds us of the spiritual principles designed to guide us into the life we desire and deserve right now, not someday. This life is here for us now!

With emphasis on listening to our own spiritual guidance, we give ourselves permission to tune into the frequency of that internal voice of Spirit within each one of us. We are inspired by the author's wisdom to commit to be all that we have come to be with faith, courage and boldness.

Author Kelley presents to us a pathway for us to experience life in a way that Thoreau described as living "with the license of a higher order of being". *Living Full-Tilt,* rather than just existing, requires commitment, courage and a mighty faith. **This book will change your life if you will let it!**

My prayer is that you will open your heart to this message of transformation, remember who you truly are and live a life of outrageous bliss!

Rev. Dr. Edwene Gaines

Author of *The Four Spiritual Laws of Prosperity*, A Simple Guide to Unlimited Abundance.

Rock Ridge Retreat Center, Valley Head, Alabama www. prosperityproducts.com

Living Full-Tilt

Affirmations

God is my Source.

I am a precious child of God and I deserve all good.

I forgive and I am forgiven for all mistakes in the past, present and future.

Nothing can keep me from my God ordained success.

God has not given me a spirit of fear but of power, love and a sound mind.

I listen within and follow as I am guided.

My good comes to me pressed down, shaken together and running over.

I now have enough time, energy, wisdom, love, and money to accomplish all of my desires.

I release all blocks and give myself permission to live the life of my dreams.

The Power that is within me is greater than any power in the world. With God all things are possible.

Everything that I could ever want is here for the asking and I live in a state of gratitude.

It is God's good pleasure to give me the kingdom. I have robust health, harmonious, balanced relationships, satisfying life activities and all of the material wealth that I can use wisely.

I give lovingly and generously. I am supplied lovingly and generously.

And so it is, Amen.

As you begin reading this book, start saying these affirmations right away. Say them at least once shortly after waking and at least once just before going to sleep. Say them aloud if possible. The sound of your own voice will help open your heart and mind to the unlimited possibilities before you. Saying these affirmations will give you a jump-start in creating a life you *love* living.

PREFACE

In this book I use the words God, Spirit, Creator, Universe, Source, Higher Power and other words and phrases meaning, the energy greater than anything. I use mostly Christian terminology because it is that which I am most familiar. Please feel free to substitute whatever words or phrases feel most comfortable to you. It is my intention to be inclusive and to open these universal principles and concepts to everyone, *no exceptions.*

Living Full-Tilt is meant to be used as a tool for a better life. You do not need to agree with every thought and concept to receive benefit from this book. Use the recommendations that work well for you and release the rest.

Disclaimer

By law, I cannot and do not guarantee specific results from using the ideas and practices outlined in this book. The results that you get depend on your experience, awareness, commitment and the level of action that you take. This book is not intended to replace counseling, therapy or medical treatment. Seek professional help when needed. With that being said, I believe in your ability to make positive changes in your life.

Follow Your Dream

"If you want to "taste the fruit of the tree you have to go out on a limb."
Shirley MacLaine (from the movie, "Out on a Limb")

"When guided by Spirit, don't be afraid to take risks. Live by Universal Principles and you cannot fail!"

Janie Kelley

Have you ever wondered what it would be like to:

- Live your life at a level that you would never have to pass up an opportunity to do, be or have anything because of money?
- Experience deep, lasting joy in your life that does not depend on circumstances or other people?
- Release all struggle and live out all of your heart's desires?
- Live a life of sheer opulence?

- Have the freedom and ability to give away significant amounts of money to help your fellow human beings?
- Be completely free to be all that you came here to be?
- Live your life from a standpoint of *freedom, joy* and *plenty*?

This book is in your hands right now because *living full-tilt* is a desire of your heart. You were probably attracted to the title of this book because it describes how you want to live your life. There are no accidents in this divinely ordered universe; therefore, you are reading this by divine appointment. You are drawn to this book because the time has come for you to **stop settling** for a mediocre, or even less than mediocre, existence. The time has come for you to stop resigning yourself to being less than you can be. **The time has come for you to live the life of your dreams!**

Congratulations!

Your time is now!

Begin Where You Are

If you want to live the life of your dreams, and you are not currently doing so, something must change. This change will require you to move out of your comfort zone. It will require that you let go of your safety net. It will require that you "go out on a limb."

It is equally important to begin where you are and be gentle with yourself as you learn and grow. Let go of criticizing yourself. Know that it is progress that you seek, not perfection.

Just as there are physical laws that govern the physical world, there are spiritual laws that govern the universe. *Living Full-Tilt* takes you through seven of these universal principles that, when practiced with regularity, will support your life of *freedom, joy* and *plenty*. The areas these principles cover are:

1. "Deservability"
2. Forgiveness
3. Gratitude
4. Giving and Receiving
5. Setting Intentions
6. Living your Purpose in Life
7. Commitment

When you learn the spiritual principles that govern these areas and put these principles to work in your life, you place yourself squarely in the flow of the good that was prepared for you even before you were born. *When guided by Spirit, don't be afraid to take risks. Live by universal principles and you cannot fail.* When you begin to put these laws into practice, much of the time your good flows to you so fast that it seems like you are living in a dream. You will have to learn to receive to a much greater degree than ever before in your life. You will have to learn to *"Increase your tolerance for pleasure."* Edwene Gaines

When you put these laws into practice your health improves, relationships harmonize, you find satisfaction in your work and life activities, and money flows to you in sufficient amounts to live a full, rich, opulent life. Whenever these areas are balanced you are free to live the life of your dreams and to be all that you came here to be! Being balanced does not necessarily mean that all areas of your life must be given equal time and attention. That can happen, but it is rare. Having your life in balance simply means giving the appropriate amount of time and energy to each segment of your life. There was a time in my life when I thought a balanced life meant that my life's work, my primary relationship, recreation, relaxation and self-care each had to have the same amount of time and attention. Now I know that, for me, a schedule like that is not only unrealistic but, impossible!

Balance means giving appropriate amounts of our time and attention to each area. The appropriate amount of time for each area may shift and change from time to time. We each get to decide.

Unconventional Claims

I may make statements and claims that defy conventional wisdom. It may be the use of conventional wisdom that brought you to your present set of circumstances. If you are to live an extraordinary life you must do extraordinary things! You must break free from much of the accepted norm. What society considers normal is often times dull, boring and lacking in imagination. In order to live the life of your dreams you must defy conventional wisdom in many situations. Much of the time, conventional wisdom leads to mediocrity. In order to live the life of your dreams you must get used to being the exception rather than the rule.

If you do what you have always done, you will get what you have always gotten. *If you wanted what you already have, most likely you would not be reading this book.* I ask that you let go of your preconceived notions about what you have been taught and all that you thought you knew about how things work. For now, open yourself and embrace the teachings in this book. This book is the accumulation of more than thirty years of study and many more years of life experience. Put these spiritual principles into practice and see the changes take place in your life. In order to know that these spiritual laws really work, you must give them an honest effort and a fair trial of *at least six months.* The positive changes will most likely come much quicker but six months will surely see a positive change if you follow closely the principles outlined in this book. After you have given the principles and suggestions a fair trial (no less than six months) you are free to pick up your old beliefs and go back to the life that you are currently living if you so choose. For now, let go of your preconceived ideas about everything.

Right now I encourage you to embrace a Zen Buddhist concept called "Shoshin" (pronounced "show-shinn"). It means "beginners mind." It refers to the letting go of preconceived ideas, beliefs and notions and being open minded as though not knowing anything, much like a small child. Observe a child between one and three years of age. They look at everything with new eyes because the whole world is new to them. A baby can be entertained for long periods of time by a simple set of keys. Small children ask lots of questions because they don't yet know about the world around them and they are curious. They don't know the names of objects and how these objects fit into *their* world. They have a beginner's mind. They are open to all possibilities and they don't know anything about limitation. As you read this book, I encourage you to practice "Shoshin".

I invite you to pretend that you know nothing about how the world works and how you are to live your life. Let these ideas, thoughts and principles fall on new ground as a seed into fertile soil. When an apple seed is placed in rich soil and given adequate water and sunshine, over time, it develops into an apple tree and eventually bears an untold number of apples. When you allow the seeds of the teachings in this book to fall on the fertile ground of your beginner's mind, in time, these ideas will produce the fruit of harmony, freedom, joy, love, peace of mind and plenty in every area of your life, including your finances!

I am living proof of it! I started my life in poverty and now I am living the life that I used to only dream of and, at one time, did not think possible. I have tested these universal laws in my own life and I know that they work.

The physical law of gravity works equally for everyone. Gravity does not care what gender or race you are, what achievements or failures you have experienced, what status you have in the community, what age you are, your degree of attractiveness or what talent you possess. Gravity works the same for everyone. No matter who you are gravity holds you to the earth. In that respect, spiritual laws are the same as gravity. *Spiritual laws of the universe work equally for everyone when observed and applied correctly.* We are each precious to God and the Universe does not play favorites. If these laws work for me, they will work for you, as well.

If Nothing Changes, Nothing Changes!

If you want your life to be different, something must change. Realistically, you cannot continue with your current attitudes, beliefs and actions and expect anything to be different. If nothing changes, nothing changes!

- If you want your life to be different, you must **do** some things differently.
- If you want your life to be different, you must **view** some things differently.

These statements may seem very simple and quite logical. They are. Some of the most profound teachings are simple and logical, yet not widely recognized in our world today. Living the life of your dreams will require that you make changes in the way that you *do* and *view* things. Some of these changes may be seemingly small and may be relatively easy to implement. These small changes, over time, will have large results. Even the smallest steps, when taken in the right place, with perseverance, will eventually take you to the top of Mount Everest. An example could be to watch less TV. I am not suggesting that you give up watching TV. It can be a good source of entertainment, relaxation and information but research shows that the average American watches six hours of TV a day. One hour less of TV a day would give you seven hours a week to pay attention to someone you love, prepare a nourishing meal, exercise; engage in a hobby, read a good book or some other productive activity. Ultimately, you have freed up 30 hours a month and 365 hours in a year just by watching 1 hour less of TV a day.

Some changes may be more challenging to implement such as a career change, ending a relationship, beginning a relationship, relocating your home or workspace. Others may simply require a different viewpoint. There are some areas that may only require a change in attitude or perception in order to make a monumental difference in your life. Let's say that there is a person in your life whom you find disagreeable in some way. Make a commitment to yourself to find at least 10 things that you like about that person, no matter how long it takes. Read this list every day for 30 days. Chances are great you will begin to view that person differently. Even if that person's behavior remains the same, the change that you have made in yourself will make your life much easier. Amazing how that works!

A Course in Miracles states, *"There is always another way of looking at this."* I have found this statement to be true. No matter what I have created in my life, no matter what life brings, I have a choice about how I will look at it and I always have a choice about how I will respond to it.

One thing is for sure; if you are dissatisfied with any area of your life it is up to you to *do* and/or *view* something differently. *If nothing changes, nothing changes.*

Some changes may be as simple as a shift in the way that you see a person or situation. For example, say you have a co-worker who has a habit of tapping her pencil on her desk while she is thinking. When she does this you become irritated. Her habit of tapping her pencil is not irritating. Tapping her pencil is a neutral act. It is your perception of her tapping her pencil that is the problem. It is you who have made a judgment that the tapping is irritating. You may think to yourself, "Anyone would be annoyed or irritated under these same circumstances." Enlisting the agreement of another person does not change the facts. Shakespeare is quoted as having said, *"Things are neither good nor bad but our thinking makes it so."* To some, the rhythmic tapping may be a soothing sound.

Some changes in our world take place within our own minds and do not require any change in the outer world. Your co-worker may never change her habit of tapping her pencil and yet you have the power within your own mind to release any negative thoughts and feelings around it. This same concept can be applied to many life situations. This is just one simple example.

Please understand I am not including abusive or destructive behavior. If you or someone you know is involved in abuse or destruction, this would need to be addressed through different channels. I am, in no way, asking you to adjust your attitude about abuse.

Some changes I propose may be uncomfortable at first until you see that they work and help move you closer to the wonderful life that you imagine for yourself. Some changes may require that you muster up all of your courage and go against what you have believed, for many years, to be true. You will amaze yourself at what you can accomplish when you release old, outworn ideas, beliefs and habits in order to work *with* spiritual principles.

Creative Energy

Financial difficulty, over a long period of time, sucks the joy out of our lives and blackens our days. When much of our creative energy goes into thinking about what bills get paid and what bills must wait, or even how we are going to be able to pay any bills at all, we have little or no creative energy left to dream; much less to create a brighter future.

When living conditions are less than adequate your creative energy is used up in dealing with how to make-do, muddle along and just plain survive. It is difficult to get into a higher vibration of creative energy if you are using up your creative energy to figure out how to pay the rent, keep gas in your car, your electricity from being turned off or how to feed your family with little or no money. When your time and energy are used up in dealing with a possible foreclosure or eviction there is little or no energy left to visualize a life of opulence and plenty for yourself and your family. I know this first hand because I have experienced each of these and many other financial difficulties in my life.

With your creative energy used up on living in survival mode, how would you ever get to the place that Abraham Maslow called "Self-Actualization" where you are living at your full potential? When you get your finances to the place that money flows into your life, in sufficient quantities, the foundation is laid so that you can move in the direction of Self-Actualization. You are, then, freed-up to be who you came to be in this world.

Perhaps you are not in a place of desperation, but you are feeling like life is passing you by. Perhaps you are stuck in a job that is not fulfilling your potential or you feel trapped in a relationship that you need to release so that you can move on. Perhaps you have creative abilities that you long to use. Sometimes, **we must give up good for great.**

Imagine, for a moment, that you are at the end of your life and on your death bed. As you look back and review your life; will you see a life well-lived? Will you see a life of mediocrity? Or, will you see a life wasted?

You are here on planet earth, at this very time, to realize your full potential and to do all that is yours to do in this life. You are here to be a Self-Actualized person. In Self-Actualization you are living at, or very near, your full potential; you are *living full-tilt.*

When your basic financial needs are met on a regular basis, creative energy is then freed up to move to a higher level of thinking and living. When you have adequate food, clothing and shelter for yourself and your family, creative ideas and robust energy are a natural result. The time and energy once spent on the struggle of seeing to the absolute necessities of survival can then be converted into positive, forward-thinking, creative energy. When basic necessities are handled with relative ease, you can avail yourself to opportunities that once were totally out of your reach. Working with universal principles will give you the raw material needed to co-create a life well-lived.

You Are Divine

God did not create you to live a life of hardship, struggle and doing without. You are made in the image and likeness of The Creator. You are a son or a daughter of The Most High! You are "A Point of Light within the Greater Light." Prosperity, of every kind, is your birthright!

You are a spiritual being living in a human body and your basic purpose here on earth is to experience your divinity and express your divinity.

You are not experiencing divinity or expressing divinity by living a life of hardship, struggle, and doing without. You experience and express your divinity when you live a life of *freedom, joy* and *plenty*. These statements are not meant to evoke guilt. That would only compound the problem. These statements are to help you see that you are meant for greater things!

When you learn to live your life filled with opulence and generosity, you glorify your Creator. By doing so, you silently teach others to do the same. That is not to say that you will never encounter challenges. Challenges will come, but you will deal with them from a higher level of consciousness. Dealing with challenges is different from living a life of hardship. When living a life of freedom, joy and plenty you will be faced with occasional challenges. You may have an unexpected expense that presents an opportunity to expand your prosperity consciousness. You may lose a loved one and spend time in grief. You may lose a job and grieve that loss, as well. Challenging situations will come. Remember, they are temporary.

Living a life of hardship is an over-arching condition of perceived lack and limitation that defines your whole life. A life of hardship affects relationships, work, health, money and life in general. You were not meant to live a life of hardship.

Many of us have been taught to believe that it is more spiritually acceptable or even preferable to have very few possessions, little money and to barely get by. Somehow, we have embraced the idea that this way of living is honoring to God. This is simply not true.

"For I know the plans that I have for you," declares the Lord, "plans to prosper you and not to harm you; plans to give you hope and a future." Jeremiah 29:11 (NIV)

"Fear not little flock for it is the Father's good pleasure to give you the kingdom." Luke 12:32 (KJV)

"Ask and it shall be given you…" Matthew 7:7 (KJV)

"Honor is the very root of wealth." Hinduism

"He who does what is proper, who takes the yoke upon him and exerts himself, will acquire wealth." Buddhism

What if you had lots of money to distribute any way that you saw fit? Just think of the ways that you will honor God when you are in charge of great wealth! You will then have an opportunity to give educational scholarships, build hospital wings, fund food banks, build parks for families, contribute to libraries, start businesses that create jobs, support ministries and spiritual leaders, rescue animals, give monetary gifts to loved ones, etc. You fill in the blanks because the list is endless. It is up to you to determine how your wealth is distributed. Much good can be achieved when your financial wealth is used wisely.

The more we give the more we receive. As Ralph Waldo Emerson said, "You cannot out-give God." I agree. How much fun do you think it might be to test that theory?

Living Full-Tilt

What does *Living Full-Tilt* mean? A dictionary states that "living" means; "active, thriving, vigorous and strong". A dictionary definition of "full-tilt" is this: "to the highest potential." When we put the two definitions together, *Living Full-Tilt* means; *"A life that is active, vigorous and strong being lived to the highest potential"*.

What does it mean to live your life "active, vigorous, strong and to the highest potential?" For as many people as there are on earth, there is probably that same number of descriptions. You get to make up your own meaning.

What does "actively living to the highest potential" mean to you? Stop reading for a few minutes and take out a sheet of paper and finish this sentence, "Now that I am actively living at my highest potential, I am................." Be sure to include the four major areas of life; health, relationships, money and career/life activities. As you do this exercise, let go of things that you see as limitations such as; age, race, gender, education, living conditions, current job, physical ability, money, etc. Do not look to conditions for what seems possible. For this exercise release ALL perceived limitations. Forget about what you think is possible and let your imagination run free! Even if you cannot see how it could ever happen, write it down.

One of my favorite lines from Edwene Gaines is, *"How is none of your business!"* Do this exercise now.

Welcome Back! When you learn spiritual principles and how to cooperate with them, a whole new world of higher consciousness will open up to you. You will learn the advantages of working with the laws of prosperity and, in doing so, riches will manifest around you to support you as you do your work in the world. When you learn and practice spiritual principles, such as The Law of Giving and Receiving, the promise is that God will "open the windows of heaven and pour you out a blessing that there is not room enough to receive it." Malachi 3:10 (KJV)

I will share, with you, my personal definition of *Living Full-Tilt*. My detailed definition has changed over time and I expect it will continue to change as I move along in life and grow spiritually. However, the five basics remain the same.

My definition of *Living Full-Tilt* is:

- A moment by moment relationship with my Creator
- Robust health of body and mind that enables me to be all that I came here to be and do all that is mine to do
- Harmonious, nurturing and balanced relationships
- Satisfying work and life activities
- All of the material wealth that I can use wisely

Each of these 5 areas is interconnected with the others. For instance:

It isn't enough to be wealthy if my health is poor and I cannot enjoy the options that money brings.

If my relationships are out of harmony, it will probably have a negative effect on my work.

If I don't like my job it will affect my relationships and my health.

If my finances are lacking, it will affect my relationships and my activity in the world.

If my relationship with God is out of alignment it will affect every area of my life.

Do you see how it works? Every area of prosperity is inter-related with every other area. When one area is brought into alignment the other areas just naturally come into better balance and vibrate at a higher frequency. A rising tide lifts all of the boats.

There is nothing that comes into your life that is isolated unto itself. Everything that enters your life affects everything else to varying degrees. It is like the proverbial ripple in the pond. If you were to throw even the smallest pebble into a pond, it would displace some of the water, creating ripples on the surface of the water, which would, in turn, move vegetation around, therefore, affecting depth of the water (if even to a minute degree). Everything that enters your life affects other areas. In order to be all that you came here to be you must begin by addressing at least one area of your life that affects how you live. You may choose to address one area at a time, more than one or all at once. The important thing is – BEGIN!

Prosperity Principles at Work

If a parachute is made using the correct standards, if it is packed properly, and if it is used properly in accordance with the directions it will always open because the principles governing the parachute work. If you have a combination lock and you use the right combination it will always open. It is the same with the principles that govern prosperity. When prosperity principles are understood and correctly applied they will always work. In order to use prosperity principles you must study them to understand them. A very important factor is this; to gain a good understanding of prosperity principles you must commit to applying them to your life. They will always work when properly understood and properly applied for *the required length of time*. The required length of time may vary; therefore, it is extremely important to persevere. It is wise to make a commitment to your dream until results are achieved. Many people make the mistake of giving up just before results are about to show up.

The Purpose of This Book

This book is the result of more than thirty years of study and a lifetime of experience in living at varying levels of the prosperity spectrum. I know what it is like to live in poverty; not only material poverty but emotional and spiritual poverty as well. I know what it is like to live the life of my dreams;

with a measure of freedom, joy and plenty. I know from personal experience that when we learn spiritual principles and abide by them we place ourselves squarely in the flow of the good that The Universe has for each of us.

This book includes timeless wisdom and practical exercises that, when applied with commitment, will place you squarely in the position to receive all that you need to live the life of your dreams. When you master money and materiality much of your creative energy is freed up to pursue your heart's desires and to be all that we came here to be. Conversely, if you are worried about how you are going to pay the bills, how you are going to buy food and provide health care for yourself and your family, your creative energy is drained, and there is very little, if any, energy left to move toward your full potential. If you are going to be a fully actualized person and reach your potential, you cannot live for long periods of time in survival mode. You must move beyond the basics of life and embrace your creative potential. With money and finances securely in place, you experience more freedom and are able to take advantage of expanded opportunities. Your mental, emotional and physical energy can be used for your higher purpose. You will "*live with the license of a higher order of being*", as Henry David Thoreau put it.

The purpose of this book is to give you the tools that you need to master money and materiality so that you are then free to move on and reach your full potential. The purpose of this book is to move you into *Living Full-Tilt.*

Freedom, Joy and Plenty

This is your handbook to freedom, joy and plenty. This book is designed to be read many times. You might want to read it through the first time to get the overall picture in your mind. Upon subsequent readings, take your time and allow yourself to apply the principles and suggestions to your life; stop and do the exercises, repeat the affirmations and allow yourself to sit with the meditations. Stop when you come to an idea or concept that really hits home. Take the steps necessary to really incorporate the principles into your life. Make these universal principles a part of who you are. It is your handbook to living a life you love!

One of my greatest joys in life is to be instrumental in helping another person to achieve a goal that moves that person in the direction of creating a life they love living. My heart sings when I can rejoice with another in the achievement of fulfilling his or her heart's desires toward a richer, freer, fuller life.

This is your life!

This is your time!

Be all that you came here to be!

Here's to *Living Full-Tilt!*

CHAPTER I

Prepare Yourself to Receive

*"I am a child of the Absolute Good. God is good
and I am good. Everything that comes into my life
is good and I am going to have only good."*

Charles Fillmore

*"I am a precious child of God and I deserve all
good".*

Janie Kelley

Your Birthright

You are a precious child of God and prosperity of every kind
is your birthright! Take a moment to allow that statement to
really sink in. Does it sound true? How does it feel? Are you
at least open to it?

It is your birthright to be rich in every area of your life. It is
your birthright because you are the offspring of a rich and
loving Creator. You were born to live a life of *freedom, joy* and

1

plenty! You are a precious expression of God, and you deserve all good!

We will now lay a solid foundation that will move you into living the life of your dreams. A house must have a strong foundation on which to build a beautiful and lasting structure that will serve its occupants well. Likewise, your life of prosperity and abundance must have a strong foundation to support the spiritual principles that will serve you well. From this strong foundation you will learn how to release old, outworn ideas, beliefs and notions that do not serve you so that new ideas, beliefs and notions may enter and become a solid part of your life.

Living a prosperous life includes money. Every area of life is affected, in some way, by money. Whether you like it or not; whether you agree with it or not, does not change that fact. Money is an important part of life because, at this point in the evolution of humankind, money is the common medium of exchange. And yet, it is one of the most difficult subjects for many people to talk about.

Rightly used, money is a means to an end not the end itself. Spiritually speaking, money helps us do good in the world and does not come into our lives just so that we can merely accumulate it. **Money is a tool not a goal.**

Money is neutral and does not care what you do with it. It is just green paper. The same million dollars can be used to build schools or bombs. Money is neutral. We determine whether money will build or destroy.

It is what we do with money that determines whether or not we live a rich, full life or simply have a lot of money. Many options are afforded us through the medium of exchange called money that would not otherwise be available. With riches in the form of money we have the opportunity to be a philanthropist and help make positive changes in people's lives. We have the opportunity to do good in the world that, without money, we would not have the same options.

"Deservability"

"Deservability" is the first foundational piece of *living full-tilt*. If you do not feel that you deserve the good that life has to offer, you will devise ways (either consciously or unconsciously) to hold your good away. Even if good comes to you it will not stay without the basic *knowing* that you deserve it.

The dictionaries that I consulted reported that "deservability" is not a word. I say it is. My definition of deservability is, "the ability to know that one is of worth and value therefore deserving". Much like a child born to a wealthy king inherits a crown and riches, you deserve good simply because you are a child of God. Open yourself to your good. As human beings we are one. I am connected with you through Divine Mind. Because of that, I can hold, for you, the affirmations in this book knowing that they are true even if you cannot believe them for yourself.

My commitment to you is this; as you read this book I will pray with you and I will hold prosperity for you in every area of your life. All you have to do is send an email to me at:

livingfulltilt@yahoo.com

Your good will come to you by "right of consciousness", meaning, your consciousness is being prepared and opening up to receive your good.

Symptoms of Undeservability

Telltale signs can accompany the thoughts and feelings of undeservability. Have you lost money or misplaced checks that were given to you. Have you, without good reason, refused monetary help that was offered to you? Have you received a gift and not allowed yourself to use it even though it would have been helpful or given you feelings of joy? Do you have gift cards in your wallet that you won't allow yourself to use? Do you allow yourself to have fun using some of your money or is it only for *serious* use? Do you deflect compliments by saying things like, "This old thing," or "It only cost ten dollars," or "Anyone could have done it?" Do you explain away compliments until they are rendered meaningless? One statement that I hear frequently is, "It wasn't me; it was God." My thought about this is that the person declaring this statement had to be open and surrendered so that God could do a good work through him or her.

Yes, give credit to God *and* allow a compliment to settle within and be absorbed, understanding that you had a significant part in it. You are how God expresses in the world.

The words that we use in ordinary conversation are quite telling. Sincere apologies are occasionally necessary to clear the air and restore harmony to a relationship. However, if we hear ourselves saying, "I'm sorry," or apologizing many times each day, it is time to take a deeper look. Words are powerful and often revealing. This habit of apologizing many times a day often comes from a deep seated feeling of unworthiness.

We may make remarks such as, "Nothing good ever happens to me," or, "Just my luck…," or, "Our family is just destined to be poor." We would do well to listen to the words we speak and the thoughts we think. Words have power. They are determining factors of our future. When thinking or speaking, we may ask ourselves, "Do I want more of what I just thought? Do I want more of what I just said?" If the answer is "no" release the thought or words and replace them with thoughts or words of what is wanted. The thoughts that we think and the words that we speak are constantly creating the life that we live. As is written in Proverbs 23:7 (KJV); "For as he thinks in his heart, so is he." Also in Proverbs, "Death and life are in the power of the tongue…" Proverbs 18:21 (KJV)

Oneness

The Creator cannot be separated from Its creation. We are one with God and one with each other as a human family. We are connected through Divine Mind.

"God, who did make the world and all things in it,…made also of one blood every nation of men to dwell upon the earth…" Acts 17:26 (YLT)

"God is the Father. Earth is the Mother. With all things and in all things, we are relative." Sioux-Native American (from the book, *Oneness*, by Jeffrey Moses)

Procrastination

Procrastination can be a symptom of undeservability. When we put off doing something that has the potential to enhance our lives, the basis of that can be rooted in undeservability. Many times, deep feelings of unworthiness are the cause of cutting off our good. We commonly call it self-sabotage. At our deepest core we may not feel that we deserve the good that life is offering to us so we procrastinate and push it away.

What is that thing in your life that you have been putting off for a long time? Maybe you have started it but not completed it. Maybe you have made several false starts and never really moved forward with it. If you were to do that thing today, or at least do something that moves you in the direction of the goal, how would that feel? Imagine the goal completed. How would the completion of that goal enhance your life? How would the completion of that goal move you in the direction of your dream? Are you procrastinating about this goal because deep-down you do not feel worthy of the good that will come as a result of it?

Albert Einstein said that if he had one hour to solve a life or death problem he would spend 55 minutes formulating the right question. Part of helping ourselves to find our answer is learning to ask the right questions. You might start with the question, "What will my life be two years from now if I *do not* pursue my dream?" When envisioning the answer how does it make you feel? Now ask yourself the question, "What will my life be two years from now if I *do* pursue my dream?" When envisioning the answer how does that make you feel? If you continue breathing for the next two years you will create a life of some kind. Which of your answers do you want to be your reality?

When we feel undeserving, many times we will not move forward on a project or situation that will make our life better in some way. We find numerous reasons not to get started or we can't complete it. Many times the feelings of undeservability are so deep and insidious that we don't recognize them for what they are. We have lived with them for so long that they become blind spots. We may need the help of a trusted friend or counselor to help us see them. It is worth the effort because it may be the very thing hindering us from moving forward. By its very nature, a blind spot cannot be seen without help.

"Begin with the end in mind" is a popular phrase. See in your mind's eye and feel the feelings of finishing a certain project. Allow the feelings of healthy pride to come to the forefront. Visualize the job well done and see the benefits that come to you as well as others because of your having finished this project.

Don't wait for the feeling to hit you. Sometimes we allow ourselves to become paralyzed because we wait for inspiration or we wait for the mood to strike us. Waiting for the feeling and/or the mood can be part of the problem that started the habit of procrastination. Start today on something that you have been putting off. The rewards will be worth it.

The Power of the Will

Letting go of procrastination usually takes will-power but maybe not in the usual sense. Everyone has within themselves the power of "will". We sometimes hear people say, "I have no will-power". That is a false statement that has been passed down through generations; consequently, many of us have believed it. Everyone has the power of will. It is innate within all of us. The way we choose to use this power of the will has the potential to help determine our future. We use the power of will to get out of bed in the morning. We use it to get dressed, to go off to work, to do the work that is set before us, to shop for food after work, to take care of the children, to write a book, to paint a painting, to drive from one place to the other, etc. We "will" to do these things and we do them. Even those things that are routine are controlled by the will. We will to do our routine.

We can also use the power of the will to cease doing a certain task or avoid doing it altogether. The power of the will is always within each of us and comes into play every day. It is our choice as to how we use it. Just know it is a choice! The power of the will is always ready for instruction. You are using the power of your will right now. You willed to read this book.

Using the power of the will start a project that you have been putting off or complete a project that you have started. Let go of any negative thoughts that you have had in the past about it. Set a reasonable date that you intend to be finished with that project. Don't set yourself up by choosing a target date that you cannot reasonably meet. Placing unreasonable demands on yourself is another way of self-sabotage. When you fail to meet the unreasonable demand you would probably have negative feelings and thoughts about yourself. That starts a downward spiral that once again leads to procrastination.

When the project is completed you will experience such a sense of satisfaction that is far beyond the mere completion of whatever you have chosen to do. It will reinforce your sense of self-worth. Don't wait for the project to be completed to celebrate. Celebrate the small achievements along the way! The sense of satisfaction and accomplishment will go a long way in building self-confidence and the knowledge that procrastination is a choice that you make using the power of the will. You can also use that same power of the will to move past that behavior to a more satisfying way. How do you choose to use your power of will?

Childhood Issues

Maybe you have never really learned how to love yourself in a healthy way. There may have been times in your life that you have failed to receive the wonderful gifts that God has for you because, due to the lack of healthy self-love, you did not feel you deserved the good in life. You may have seen yourself as unlovable. This embedded belief probably started very early in your life. If your parents or primary caregivers did not love themselves in a healthy way, how could they teach it to you? They were able to teach and model only to the extent of their own knowledge and beliefs. If they had known a better way they would have taught you a better way.

If your parents or primary caregivers lived their lives from a place of fear, scarcity, limitation and undeservability; if they did not display healthy self-love, that is what you would naturally pick up and adopt as your own belief. They may have taught you things like:

- There is not enough to go around.
- Don't be greedy.
- You are a sinner, therefore, unworthy and undeserving.
- If you are rich, others will have to go without.
- Don't think too highly of yourself.
- Rich people are dishonest.
- Our family has always been poor.

These and many other messages have been perpetuated through generations and can keep you in a state of confusion about your innate, God-given right to be prosperous and happy.

Money is the root of all evil. This is one of the most misquoted scriptures in the Bible. The scripture actually reads, "For the *love* of money is the root of all kinds of evil." I Timothy 6:10)

Your desire to move upward and forward comes from deep within your soul. Charles Fillmore said, "Desire is the onward impulse of the ever evolving soul." It is natural to feel that upward pull from within but many have learned to feel guilty for even thinking thoughts of wealth and doing better in life let alone living a life of full-blown prosperity and happiness. Just as you learned false and negative ways of thinking you can unlearn them.

If you have lingering childhood issues, take the necessary steps to deal with them. Childhood issues may be a barrier to living the life of your dreams. If professional help is needed, by all means, see that you get it. Don't let unresolved issues stand in the way of your reaching your full potential and being all that you came here to be.

Beliefs

A belief system is simply a series of thoughts that we have repeated in our mind. That is all. No matter where these thoughts originated, if they do not work to support peace of mind and a life of joy, it is time to let them go. Just as we learned negative teachings, we can unlearn them and embrace the positive teachings of our own choice. *Simply because someone we trusted taught it to us, does not make it true.* It is time to release those teachings that do not work in our lives. It is time to replace those old negative, limiting beliefs with new, more positive ones that are life-giving!

A test that I use is this; "Does this thought or belief ultimately bring me peace of mind or joy?" If the answer is "no", I set about to look more closely at it with the idea of changing it. If the answer is "yes" I allow my mind to rest there because I know that, "Thoughts held in mind produce after their kind."

Conditioned Beings

We are each conditioned beings. We were conditioned by those around us in our early life and we believed that what they were telling us was true. We drew our conclusions about ourselves and about the world in general very early in life. Some of these conclusions serve us well while others do not. We created patterns in our lives because of the conclusions that we reached when we interpreted the words, body language and actions of the important people in our lives. Patterns and habits stem from thoughts that go through our minds based on what we have experienced. These habitual thoughts then form our belief systems that stay with us throughout our life unless we make the effort to examine what works and what doesn't work. It is a good practice to, periodically, examine our beliefs. We may want to look at beliefs such as those which we were taught about God. Chances are we may want to reinterpret some of the concepts that we were taught. If we were taught that God is angry and punishing, how do we reconcile that with the scripture that states, "God is love"? (I John 4:8 KJV) It doesn't say that God has the characteristic of love. God is the "allness" of love itself. If God is the epitome of love, how can punishment be a part of God's nature? That would require a God of duality. Could it be that human characteristics have been assigned to God? Remember, we were made in the image of God, not the other way around.

There is a Bible scripture that declares, "Test everything, hold fast to what is good" (I Thessalonians 5:21 RSV). For me, this is an invitation to "hold up to the light" any teaching or information that I have received, be it spiritual or otherwise, and see how it works in my life today. If a teaching does not work in my life, it is of no help to me. As I evolve spiritually, my understanding changes. Simply because a person or a group of people make a declaration that certain spiritual beliefs are "truth" does not make it so. Remember, there was a time when it was believed that the Earth stood still while the sun came up over it in the morning and in the evening went down under it. Just because a theory or teaching is believed by the masses does not make it true. *"Test everything", including, the teachings in this book.*

We would do well to trace back to the origin of some of our erroneous beliefs so that we can "look them squarely in the eye", make peace with them and release them. We do that so that we can go on to live the life of peace, joy and opulence that God intended us to live.

Loving Yourself is Essential

Loving yourself is not only the basis of deservability but it must be addressed in order to live the life of your dreams. No amount of money, achievements or relationships can make up for the lack of healthy self-love. You must be willing to do whatever it takes to get to the place of loving yourself in a healthy way. Healthy self-love is essential, not optional, in building the life of your dreams.

In order to feel deserving of riches, good health, satisfying work and harmonious relationships we must move toward loving ourselves unconditionally. We must take steps to heal the thoughts and feelings responsible for telling us that we are not worthy of love. We are looking to gain insight into thoughts and behaviors. *We are not looking to blame anyone, especially ourselves, because* **blame is a never-ending game in which there are no winners.**

When we trace back to the root cause, we will find that we were not born with feelings of unworthiness. We were taught to feel that way by the words, actions and attitudes of those around us as we were growing up. This is not to hunt down someone to name as the culprit because those around us were doing what they knew to do based on the information and experience that they had at the time. If we knew more about their childhoods, we would probably understand that, for the most part, they taught us what they had been taught. If they had it to do over today, those same people would probably teach us differently. As they have gained insight and experience, their lives are different. Therefore, what they teach and model would be different. At the time they were probably doing what they thought would help us get along well in life. They were giving us the best advantages that they knew how to give. That does not change the fact that, for many of us, their best efforts left us unprepared for life, or worse, it left us wounded. It not only left us unprepared and wounded, in most cases, it left us not knowing what to do to change the negative patterns that had been deeply established.

In our society it is perfectly acceptable to love another person. We are not, as a general rule, taught to love ourselves in a healthy way. We are sometimes taught to love others to the point of sacrificing our own health, wealth and happiness. In the minds of some, this is somehow thought to be commendable. We may be criticized or looked down upon if we "think too highly of ourselves". This is one of the areas in which we would do well to let go of conventional wisdom.

Unless you love yourself first you cannot give genuine love to another person. You can only love another to the degree that you truly love yourself. You cannot give what you do not have. If you wanted to give $50 to another person you must first have the $50. You cannot give $50 if you do not have $50. It is the same with love.

I am not referring to the type of pseudo self-love that takes on the form of boasting, self-centeredness and self-absorption. Traits, such as these, are created to hide the real feelings of disapproval of oneself and sometimes even self-loathing. Somewhere in the mind of the person who disapproves of him or her self, there is the belief that if they can convince others that they are lovable and worthy then they can make it true in their own minds. There is not enough approval outside them to fill the void and make self-approval true in their own minds. Healthy self-love must come from within.

When we truly love ourselves in a healthy way, it is usually a quiet, unassuming type of love. We probably would not introduce ourselves to another person and say, "Hi. My name is Janie and I love myself." (Although that might be kind of fun) People would think that very strange at best. When we have a healthy love for ourselves we don't have to announce it. We exude confidence and genuine centeredness, generally in a quiet sort of way. When we love ourselves, we often display healthy self-confidence and others will probably look to us as an example. *We silently teach people how to treat us by the way that we treat ourselves.* The healthier self-love that we have, the more genuine love and respect we will gain from others, as a general rule. A fringe benefit of loving ourselves is that we silently give others permission to do the same. Then it becomes an unending cycle of unconditional love for self and for each other.

Jesus said, "Love your neighbor as yourself." Matthew 19:19 (NLT) It is both a command and a statement. Jesus was telling the people to show love to each other in the same way that they love themselves. At the same time it was a statement. We do love others in the same way that we love ourselves. We are able to give love only to the degree that we have recognized the love that already exists within our own selves. As Eric Butterworth said, "You cannot give from your nothingness." I say, we can only give out of our "somethingness". Simply put, we can only give what we have.

Are you willing to do the work to truly love yourself? Are you willing to be healed of old, outworn ideas and beliefs? Are you willing to do whatever it takes to live the life of your dreams? I believe the answer is "yes" because you have read this far in this book. Here are some practices that will strengthen your healthy self-love:

1. Remind yourself often that you are made in the image and likeness of God.
2. Remind yourself often that God loves you unconditionally.
3. Surround yourself with loving, emotionally healthy people.
4. Meditate on seeing yourself as God sees you.
5. Read material that supports healthy self-love.
6. Take excellent physical, emotional and spiritual care of yourself.
7. Set and maintain healthy personal boundaries.
8. Step into living your life as though you already are the person you aspire to be.

Meditation on Love

Sit quietly and close your eyes. Set an intention to open your heart and mind and surrender to the God of your understanding. God loves you with a love so great that it cannot be completely grasped and understood by human beings. It is always safe to surrender to God. Allow yourself to feel the love of God surrounding you, enfolding you and infusing you. If you are a visual person you may picture yourself being enveloped by huge, loving arms. If you are not particularly visual, you may want to allow yourself to feel the feelings of the deepest love that you have ever known. Ask to feel yourself being enfolded in unconditional love. Allow yourself to take in as much as you can, knowing that each time that you sit with this love, your grasp of it will become stronger and stronger. Hold these thoughts and feelings for as long as you can. When you are ready, open your eyes and resume your day.

Do this exercise when you are aware of feelings of unworthiness. This short meditation will bring you closer and closer, in consciousness, to the unconditional love of God that is always available to you. With each session you will learn more of who you really are; A Precious Expression of God, a Child of the Universe, A Point of Light within the Greater Light or any phrase works best for you.

What is Money?

At this point in the evolution of humankind, money is the most common medium of exchange. It is a symbol of energy. Simply put, you perform a service (expend energy) for which you are paid money (a symbol of energy expended). You then take that money and give it to other people and companies for goods and services. Money represents the energy that you expended and is easy and convenient to exchange. Before our system of money was in place there was the barter system. If you were a chicken farmer you would take eggs and chickens to the person who owned the flour mill. You would then exchange the eggs and chickens for flour to make bread. The owner of the mill would then take the eggs and chickens that he had received from you and either use them for himself or exchange them for vegetables from a nearby farmer, and so on. Money is much more convenient than carrying around chickens, eggs, vegetables or sacks of flour. Money is a convenient medium of exchange.

Paper money, simply put, is a representation of energy that has been expended. This money is then used for goods and services that are products of the energy of others. And so goes the cycle. This is a simple explanation about money and energy.

Money is meant to be in circulation. Energy is meant to circulate. In order for energy to continue to flow within us, our bodies must move and exercise on a regular basis. If we become sedentary, we lose energy. Just like our physical bodies, money is meant to move and circulate. If the money/energy is stopped or gets dammed-up in any way, it stops the flow. Water must flow or it becomes stagnate and rancid. In order for us to stay in the flow of God's good we must release a portion of our money into circulation. This does not mean that we are not to have savings accounts and investments. It means that we are not to hoard money simply for the sake of having lots of money. We are to use wisdom in the distribution of the money with which we are entrusted.

If you are going to live the life of your dreams, money will, most likely, play an important role. Money allows you to take advantage of opportunities that make for a life of expansion as opposed to a life of limitation and contraction. Comedian, Chris Rock said it every well, "Being wealthy is not so much about the stuff you can buy. It is knowing that you have options."

How Large is Your Receptacle?

Much of the time God wants more for you than you will allow yourself to receive. When standing under the "waterfall" of blessings that God has for you, do you hold a thimble, a cup, a bucket or a pipeline?

The Bible states "It is God's good pleasure to give you the kingdom". Luke 12:32 (KJV) Jesus said, "…the kingdom of God is within you". Luke 17:21 (KJV) It is your job to receive "the kingdom" using the largest receptacle possible. If your receptacle is anything other than a pipeline it is time to take the necessary steps to move to a larger receptacle. When we use a receptacle that is not open ended, we seriously limit the good that comes to us. If we use a closed end receptacle, once our receptacle is full, we cut off the flow. We are entitled to limitless good because of our birthright as expressions of The Most High. It is your job to reach out and take hold of the good that God is constantly shoving in your direction.

"Submit to God and be at peace with him. In this way prosperity will come to you." Job 22:21 (NIV)

Self-Reliance

The Buddha taught that suffering is caused by grasping and attachment. This grasping and attachment causes us to hold onto material things, ideas, notions, beliefs and relationships that have outlived their purpose or that no longer serve us in a positive way. We must take the time necessary to identify our attachments and do the work necessary to release them.

Underlying the feeling of undeservability is fear. There is the fear of letting go of material objects afraid that we might need them some day. But the deepest fear is that we might need the object and not be able to buy it (whatever the "it" may be). Having "things" around us can give a false sense of security. There is something about the familiar that tells us that everything is going to be alright. If we keep our things, we do not have to face the grief connected to the letting go that may trigger a whole new set of unknowns. A basic human fear is fear of the unknown. This is one of the factors in the Hoarding Syndrome for which professional help may be required.

We sometimes hold onto relationships, even when we know that they are over, thinking that these relationships are the best that we can do. We may think that we don't deserve anything better. Sometimes we cling to a relationship long after the life is out of it and the relationship is squeezing the life out of us. Many times we do this because at least it is familiar and we do not have to face the unknown. We don't know what it would be like to live life without the other person and the very thought of it may bring up fear, even terror.

There is also the fear of being alone. Living a solitary life (even temporarily) can bring up deep-seated fears of abandonment. Then there are the fears of not being attractive enough, smart enough, witty enough, rich enough, interesting enough, or thin enough, etc. to find another partner. One of the biggest fears of being alone seems to be the question of what may come up in that aloneness. There is the possibility of facing the issues that may require some work. A truth to remember at this point is that we are equipped to handle anything that may arise. It may be uncomfortable or downright ugly but we have within us the necessary strengths to deal with whatever may come up and we emerge a stronger, more self-reliant person.

An advantage to being alone and looking within is that we very often see positive traits and strengths that we did not know existed within us. We most likely will find ourselves to be a lot more lovable and self-reliant than we had ever imagined. That was the case with me when my marriage ended. At that point in my life, my children had reached young adulthood and were no longer living with me. I found myself living alone for the very first time in my entire life. After the initial numbness and devastation of the end of the marriage, the thought suddenly occurred to me one day, "I am completely alone". For a week, I vacillated between low-grade anxiety and full-blown panic. All sorts of scenarios went through my mind. What if I need to buy a car and there is no one to help me? What if the water pipes freeze and burst; what will I do? What if I need to travel a long distance and I have to go alone? What if I get sick in the night and there is no one here to take care of me? Then it happened. Late one night, I was driving home when suddenly there was a strange thumping noise coming from under my car. My tire had picked up a nail and was flat. I was more than a mile from home on a long, dark stretch of highway with very few houses. I lived in a somewhat rural area at the time. This was before cell phones were common. I became very frightened and begin to pray. "Dear God, why did this happen? Why couldn't it have waited until I turned in my driveway? What am I going to do? What if my car is stolen while it is parked on the side of the road? What if a criminal stops and forces me into a car? What if…What if…What if…" I was just plain scared! I did the only thing I could think to do; I picked up my purse, got out of the car, locked it and began the long hike home. It may not have felt so long except that I had on my brand new, high-heel boots. They were sassy-looking but definitely not walking shoes. Over and over I prayed one of my favorite scriptures, "God has not given me a spirit of fear but of power, love and a sound mind. God has not given me a spirit of fear but of power, love and a sound mind. God has not given me…" II Timothy 1-7 (KJV) That walk in the dark enhanced my prayer life greatly! In spite of my fear I arrived home safely feeling a heightened sense of relief and gratitude. Except for the pain in my feet I was fine. I called a local garage that had 24 hour service and explained what had happened. They came out, replaced the tire, picked me up at my home and took me to retrieve my car. That was a defining moment in my life. It was then that I "turned a corner" and began to learn that I could take care of myself. I had never been alone to take care of a situation such as a flat tire in the middle of the night. It was then that I began to realize that, no matter what happened, I would figure out what to do about it. After that experience, when I faced much larger issues, I had an inner knowing that there was nothing in life that could not be handled. "God has not given me a spirit of fear but of power, love and a sound mind." I knew then, **"For every problem there is a solution".** In the years after that incident I still went through some very difficult times when I would temporarily lose sight of my God-given strength. However, I was never far from the memory of that defining moment, with the flat tire in the dark of night.

You have that same resource within you! Whatever happens in your life, always know that God "will never leave you or forsake you". Deuteronomy 31:6 (NIV) I am reminded of a saying that I heard many years ago; "People are like tea bags. You never know how strong they are until they get into hot water."

In the years that I was single and living alone (except for my two rescue dogs) I learned how to take care of numerous life situations and how to do many repairs and projects that I would have otherwise never learned. Being single revealed a depth of strength that had always been within me, a depth of strength that I did not know I had. Until then, I was never really forced to use it. I feel exceedingly grateful for those years of being single and finding myself in positions that beckoned me to reach deeper and soar higher. They helped me to be the strong, self-reliant person that I am.

In much of our society we are taught that being alone is to be incomplete. I am happy to see this notion is changing. There was a movie some years back with a famous line in it. The leading man told his romantic partner, "You complete me." This sums up the way that most of us have been conditioned to think. We are given the subtle and sometimes not so subtle message that somehow we are broken, inferior or incomplete if we are not paired-up with another person. We take on the belief that, by ourselves, we are not enough. I have known people who will not go to a movie, a restaurant or to any public gathering unless there is someone to go with them. I am aware that some of this might stem from being an extravert who gets energy from being with people. But, I can't help but think that much of that kind of decision stems from the thought of how they may be looked upon; as incomplete.

The truth is this, you are whole and complete as a singular person. There is nothing that needs to be added that will make you more complete than you are right now. You may learn new skills and evolve into new ways of thinking and being but nothing will make you more perfect than you are at this moment. **You are enough!**

We may fear a new relationship because it brings with it many unknowns. Will the other person like me for who I really am? Will I really like the other person? Do we have enough in common? Will it last? Will my family and friends approve of him/her? And, the list is endless. There are many reasons that we hold onto worn-out or outgrown relationships. This concept can apply to our friends as well as a romantic partner. Sometimes it is for the good of all involved to release a relationship. "People come into our lives for a reason, a season or a lifetime" (from the poem, "Reason, Season, Lifetime" Author Unknown). Not all relationships are meant to last a lifetime. Once we have completed the purpose for which we came together, the healthiest thing may be to go our separate ways.

Standing on "New Legs"

Many years ago, when I first began to learn spiritual principles that were new to me, it seemed mind boggling. Among the many spiritual principles to which I was introduced, was the power of the spoken word. As the Bible says, "Death and life are in the power of the tongue." Proverbs 18:21 (KJV)

There have probably been many times in your life when someone's words moved you to feel good about yourself or reduced you to sadness and feelings of being "not enough". Our words are powerful and can build up or destroy.

I, also, learned the Spiritual Principle; "Thoughts held in mind produce after their kind." Here are other ways of saying the same thing:

- What we think about, we bring about.
- What we focus on expands.

- Whatever we place our attention on grows stronger in our lives.
- Like attracts like.

This is known as The Law of Attraction. I learned that thoughts are things and words are powerful. I learned that my thoughts and words help to create my life. This was all brand new to me and this information could not have come at a better time. This all happened many years ago but I remember clearly that I was at a critical time in my life. I was being treated for serious depression and I was suicidal. At that time, I would have the recurring, seemingly uncontrollable thought, "Life is too hard. Life is too hard. Life is too hard…" Even with that thought rolling over and over in my mind; I was still desperately searching for something, anything, to hold on to. I was searching for a reason to live. My life is precious to me now. I have a deep, inner knowing that, no matter the appearance of outside circumstances, every problem has a solution, I am enough, everything is temporary and "With God, all things are possible".

When I was introduced to the importance of thoughts and words in my life, at first I thought, "If that is true, then my negative thoughts and negative words have created this terrible mess." At that time, my mind went to guilt and shame because I had created a life that I no longer wanted to live. Then after days or maybe weeks of wallowing in self-pity, it occurred to me that if my thoughts, words and actions had created the life that I had at that time, I had the power to create a better life for myself through my thoughts, words and actions. At the time I did not know how to change my thoughts and words but I realized that I had found a potential way out of my misery. I continued to seek a way out of this black hole that I had created for myself and I slowly began to develop the necessary skills. I searched out books, workshops, groups and programs that would help me. Every single day of my life, for more than two years, I went to Twelve-Step meetings, group therapy sessions, individual therapy sessions, church or spiritually based gatherings. Some days I even attended two or three. I was determined to change my life. Through these things, I saved my life. I was like a sponge. I read everything I could get my hands on about living a positive, fulfilling life. Many aspects of my life changed in those years including the will to live. Eventually, I even developed a spark of excitement about what life might bring. Now, I live my life in gratitude and a sense of awe about what wondrous adventure will come next! These days, many mornings when I awaken I say (in my mind), "Good morning God! What wonderful things are we going to do today?"

During that very unstable time in my life I had a friend that I will call "Carrie" (not her real name). We had been friends for about 5 years prior to my embarking upon this whole, new way of life. We had spent many hours commiserating with each other about how terrible the world was, how inconsiderate most people were, how unfairly we were being treated, how awful men were, and how life, in general, was unbearable. As I look back now, I see that the basis of our relationship was misery. Dissatisfaction and the "Ain't It Awful" game were the bonds that held our friendship together. When I really *got it* that my words and thoughts were contributing to my physical illness, depression and lack of motivation to continue to live, I set about to make some changes. I worked very diligently on the words that came out of my mouth and the thoughts that seemed an endless stream of negativity. I began to notice that when I was with Carrie the conversation still took the same negative course. I would try to move our conversations in a different direction but I didn't seem to make much headway. I was very new to the concept of positive thinking and co-creating with God through my thoughts, words and actions. Metaphysically speaking, I was like a newborn baby deer. I would make an attempt to stand up but my new legs would not hold me for long. I began to avoid spending time with Carrie. When I did talk to her, I would walk away feeling that I had lost all of the positive energy that I had managed to build up within myself prior to talking with her. I felt like it was detrimental to my health and my very life itself to continue to have contact with Carrie so I made a very difficult decision. I ended the friendship. I felt that in order to save my life, literally, I could not be with her. I stopped calling her, I didn't return her calls and eventually she stopped calling. She probably never knew what happened. I felt very sad about it but, at that time; I had no life skills that would help me speak openly to her and deal with the situation. Nothing in my life had taught me how to stay in the friendship and continue to move in a positive direction with my own life. I had no skills with which to approach her in a loving way and talk to her concerning the difficulty I was having with our friendship. I did the best thing I knew to do at the time and that was to end the relationship. Now, I look back on it and I know that if a similar thing happened today, I would handle it much differently. I would set aside a time to speak candidly and lovingly to the other person and try to resolve the situation and remain friends. I have come a long way in the last few years and I have learned many more life skills. I look back and see that there were definitely things that Carrie and I needed to do together and ways that we needed to help each other. Carrie was in my life for a reason and a season but not for a lifetime. I look back on our time together and realize that I could have come no other way. My time with her helped to shape my life today; the life for which I am so very grateful. From time to time, I wonder where she is and what she might be doing. I say a prayer that she is happy with her life.

We sometimes hold onto ideas that no longer serve us. For instance, when we were children, for our own safety, we were taught not to talk to strangers. It served us well and kept us safer than we probably would have been otherwise. Now that we are adults the rules have changed. As adults, we talk to many strangers. I find it is fun to strike up a conversation with someone while standing in line, sitting on a plane, at the gas pump or a similar situation. I never know what interesting people I am going to meet that way. Sometimes we continue to hold onto rules that served us well for a time but are no longer useful. We may have a tendency to continue to hold onto ideas and beliefs because it is all that we know. There may be religious and spiritual beliefs that were taught to us early in life that we continue to adhere to even though they do not really work in our lives. Sometimes we hold to them for fear of being ostracized by our family, friends, coworkers or even mere acquaintances. We may secretly harbor a different set of beliefs than those around us and we do not feel that we can be forthcoming with our new set of beliefs for fear of rejection.

We sometimes hold onto ideas and beliefs that never did serve us but someone in our past told us they were true and we accepted them not knowing that we had a choice. Especially when we were children, we took on the notions and beliefs of those people whom we loved and respected. As innocent children, it may not have occurred to us to question them. We simply emulated them.

Over time, we may be able to take a stand and declare our current beliefs. Sometimes life affords us an opportunity to do so disguised as a challenge. Sometimes in life we are faced with changes of such magnitude that it causes us to examine everything about life. The Universe sometimes helps us by allowing us to stir things up so much in our lives that we question everything. If we temporarily lack the courage and skills to move forward, the Universe will rise up to help us on our way. Such an occurrence happened to me. A series of events happened that caused me to question everything about my life, including the religious and spiritual teachings that I had received beginning in childhood.

In a matter of about two years amazing amounts of change took place in my life. I started a new job, opened a business with a partner (in addition to the new job), bought an existing business in addition to the one that I had opened, got divorced, had threats made on my life, I bought out my business partner, was diagnosed with a life-threatening illness, my two oldest children grew into young adulthood and went away to college and I got remarried. During that period of time, my mother went into the hospital on my birthday and died a few months later without ever returning home. The following year my father went into the hospital, again on my birthday, and died a few months later, never having returned home. There were many other changes that occurred in that two-year span of time. These are just some of the major ones. My world, as I had known it, was upside down. One day, as I drove into my driveway, an odd thought suddenly occurred to me. Over the past two years everything in my life had changed except my house and my car! The life-altering changes came so rapidly that I did not have time to process one change before another one popped up, and another and another. I didn't understand it at all. Why was this happening? My whole world was spinning out of control. I felt like I had no solid ground on which to stand! I began to question everything. I was at a point in my life that I had lost so many things I felt like I had very little of real value left to lose. I felt lost, abandoned and useless. The rules that governed my life no longer worked and I felt "set out to sea." Every day seemed replete with problems and completely different than the day before. When my feet touched the floor in the morning I would feel dread in the pit of my stomach because I had no idea what difficulties to expect that day. Every day brought a multitude of problems. I thought to myself, "Is there really a God? Or, is that just a made-up concept so that people will be afraid not to be "good" and follow the rules? If there is a

God, why are so many terrible things happening to me?" I felt like I had no foundation for my life. I thought, "What kind of God would allow all of these things to happen to me that are making me so miserable?" For most of my life, my church and my spiritual life have been very important to me and yet questions came pouring out of me with no satisfying answers in sight. I threw my Bible in a drawer and quit going to church. I turned my back on my religious beliefs. I quit praying. I mentally crossed my arms and thought to myself, "If I am in this alone, then I will just go it alone. I am the only one I can rely on, anyway." That attitude only made me more fearful, depressed and lonely.

After a time I found myself talking to "something" just like I would talk to you. It bore no resemblance to prayer, at least not the way I had been taught to pray. There were no holds barred (to use a wrestling term) in what I had to say. There was crying, yelling, hand gestures and lots of difficult questions. Then when I would settle down, there would be the tiniest opening in my heart. I realized that I was talking to the God of my understanding. I did not use the formal steps or methods of prayer that I had been taught in the past. There was nothing proper about my approach to this "new" God. I just talked to a Higher Power much like I would talk to a human being. I thought that if there really was an all-knowing God, He/She/It would not be at all surprised at my thoughts and feelings anyway. That was the beginning of my new relationship with the power greater than anything that I call God. My understanding of God is as unique as my fingerprints. So is yours.

The spiritual questions in my mind continued like a raging flood. Many questions came up that, prior to this time; I would not allow myself to ask. I found no answers to my deepest questions. Many of my former teachings made no sense. I began exploring other Christian denominations for answers and a place I could call my spiritual home. I discovered many wonderful teachings but found no real fit. When that didn't work for me, I attended meetings and studied with Buddhists, Baha'i's, Taoists, Native Americans, Earth-based religions and some deeply spiritual groups of people that did not affiliate themselves with any particular religion. What I found is that God is in, but not limited to, each of these religious expressions. God has created every human being as a perfect and precious expression, no exceptions. It is human beings who have created the illusion of separation and difference. We may not always act from that place of perfection because we have free will, but perfection is always who we really are. God, who is the "allness" of love, would not create a world full of people and then place favor on only a small percentage of those people and doom the rest. There are many ways to know Our Creator. Much of the time, the religion that we practice has more to do with where we are born than anything else. Many of the world's problems come from thinking that the way we were taught early in our lives is the only way to God. Having my world broken apart was one of the hardest, most difficult, most valuable and precious experiences that I have ever had. By having my life "hit bottom", I came up questioning everything. I left no stone unturned, as they say. My life has been incredibly enriched for having that time of spiritual exploration. It helped me to form my own foundation of spiritual beliefs and not necessarily the ones passed down to me. Because of the time in my life that I chose to "test everything" I came out of it standing on "new legs".

The Vacuum Principle of Prosperity

The Vacuum Principle is this:

Letting go of old habits, outgrown relationships, and material possessions that no longer serve us creates a vacuum. Something will move in to fill the vacuum since "nature abhors a vacuum". We would do well to fill the space with healthy habits, nurturing relationships, expansiveness and enough material possessions to allow us to be who we came to be in this world.

Once we have let go of habits, relationships and material possessions, something will move in to fill the space because that is a law of nature. That is why we need to get busy filling the space with that which will serve us. The law of nature requires that something fill it. It is important to fill the space with that which serves us to be who we came here to be.

When we let go of an unwanted habit, it is important to replace it with a healthier one. For example, if constant negative thinking is a habit that you would like to eliminate, it is important to replace a negative thought with a more positive one.

We must let go of unhealthy relationships to make room in our life for healthy, nurturing ones that enhance our happiness.

Notice I used the word *enhance*, not *make*, because there is no person on the face of this Earth that has the power to make someone else happy. Happiness is a choice that we make for ourselves. True happiness comes only from within one's own self. Others can add to our happiness but no one has the power to make us happy. Abraham Lincoln said, "Folks are about as happy as they make their minds up to be." Smart man, that Honest Abe!

We must let go of material possessions we do not use in order to create a vacuum that we consciously fill with those things that we do want and that will enrich our lives. First of all, material possessions that we are not using take up physical space in our environment and can cause clutter in our homes, offices and vehicles. More importantly, if we are not currently using an object, it drains a certain amount of our energy just to have it around. Everything is made of energy and energy needs to flow. On a more practical level, we may be holding onto an article, that we haven't used in years, that would greatly enhance the life of another person. If everyone on earth took out everything that was not being used and had one giant Swap Meet no one on Earth would have to buy much, if anything at all, for years! Wouldn't that be fun!

When we hold onto a thing it fills our living space or work space and silently tells the universe, "I have all that I can hold. Don't send me anything more".

In order to open our space and our lives to the new, exciting gifts that the universe has for us, we must abide by the Vacuum

Principle of Prosperity. In order to fill our lives with the relationships, ideas and material goods that would enhance our lives, we must first get rid of what we do not want or use to make room for what we do want and what we will use. We must create space for what we expect to arrive. In a healthy environment, new, more useful things can show up with ease if space is created for them.

If we are to welcome new, more useful ideas, we must release the ones that are not useful to us. If our minds are crowded with old, outworn ideas where will we put the new ones?

If we hold onto relationships that are outgrown, destructive or unhealthy, how will we have room for the new ones which would greatly enhance our life? We must release those relationships and make a clean sweep so that space is available in our lives for the new and exciting ones.

We must rid ourselves of all material goods that we are not currently using to make way for that which we will use. We must clean out our closets, drawers, cabinets, garages, storage spaces, offices and vehicles to make space for energy to move. Our inner lives reflect our outer lives and our outer lives reflect our inner lives. Crowded physical space indicates crowded mental space and vice versa.

Consider reading a book or taking a workshop on Feng Shui. It is the ancient Chinese art of placement that helps to balance energies. According to ancient recorded history, the art of Feng Shui is 5,000-7,000 years old. It is becoming increasingly popular worldwide.

The first Feng Shui workshop that I attended the presenter started by saying, "The first three rules of Feng Shui are as follows, Number One-Declutter, Number Two-Declutter and Number Three-Declutter!" It is of paramount importance to release material possessions that we are not currently using.

You might enlist the help of a friend in the process of clearing out and rearranging your home. Afterward, you can help your friend. It can seem like less work and more fun when doing this important step with another person. Hiring a professional organizer is also an option.

I am a very visual person. I have visions of Our Creator just shoving good things (both tangible and intangible) in our direction while constantly saying, "Here you are, my Precious Child. Take these gifts and be happy". If you, being earthly parents, want to give good gifts to our children, how much more does God want to give good gifts to you. It is our job to ask, make room, and allow the good to come in.

Charles Fillmore, a co-founder of The Unity Movement, wrote, "It is perfectly logical to assume that a wise and competent Creator would provide for the needs of his creatures in their various stages of growth." Would a wise and loving Creator place desires in your heart and then withhold what is needed to fulfill those desires? Of course not! Just think about your own children or someone that you love very much. Would you show them something wonderful, convince them of how great it would be to have it and then tell them, "Too bad you don't have what it takes to get it". Of course you wouldn't!

"How much more does God want to give good gifts to those who ask?" God places desires in your heart and then delights in seeing those desires fulfilled.

Right of Consciousness

"...with God, all things are possible." Mark 10:27 (KJV)

There is nothing outside the reach of God. We live in a world of abundance and opulence. If all of the world's resources were evenly distributed to every man, woman, and child, there would be plenty of everything and with a surplus. The problem is not lack. The problem is distribution. I am not advocating a "take from the rich and give to the poor" type of solution. That would not work long term anyway. In a relatively short period of time the major portion of the earth's wealth would be back in the hands of the formerly rich and many of the same people who had experienced lack would, once again, be poor. We have all heard and read the stories of people who win the lottery, receive an inheritance or in some way come into a large sum of money only to lose it in five years or less and are back where they started, perhaps even worse off than before. When a person's consciousness has expanded along with a sense of deservability such gifts as a large sum of money, it will usually stay with the person.

Whatever we have must be ours by right of consciousness or we will likely not keep it. The term "right of consciousness" means openness of mind and heart that causes expansiveness and readiness to receive.

A solution would be to raise the consciousness of each individual person on our planet. Such is the nature of my work and my calling. I am committed to helping raise the abundance consciousness of planet Earth.

One very important way that we raise our consciousness is through meditation. When we sit in meditation we make stronger our conscious contact with the God of our understanding. With this stronger conscious connection we find peace, joy, love, compassion, abundance and similar qualities that are innate within us. We all have them. There are no exceptions. We don't always act from these qualities; we may not know how to act from these qualities, but they are within us nevertheless. When we meditate regularly, with each sitting we become more and more acquainted with the Holy Spirit within and therefore the qualities manifest themselves in our daily lives in stronger and stronger ways. Because we are all connected with each other, when the consciousness of one person is raised it helps to raise the consciousness of our entire planet, to some degree. When we continue to do this we will eventually reach the tipping point and the world, as we know it, will shift. When this shift occurs we will live at a level that, heretofore, has been only a dream in the minds of some of us. We will "live with the license of a higher order of being". Henry David Thoreau.

God is not a being who has the traits of love, compassion, peace, joy, grace, etc. God is the allness of these traits. God is love. God is peace. God is compassion. God is joy. We are made in God's image. When we meditate regularly and simply focus our attention on the God of our understanding, it cannot help but raise our consciousness. Imagine our world if everyone practiced some form of meditation on a regular basis!

Some other ways to raise the consciousness would be to study mind expanding/heart opening material, attend classes, workshops and gatherings of like-minded people. These things have the potential to increase awareness. Allow Spirit to expand your ways of thinking.

Energy Vibration

Many quantum physicists believe that everything that appears to be solid matter is, indeed, not solid at all. Everything in our world is mostly "empty space." We are energy and we vibrate at a certain rate according to our predominant thoughts, words and actions. We have a certain vibration that attracts to us people, objects and situations that are of a similar vibration and we call this a "vibrational match." If we think mostly positive thoughts and our words are mostly positive in nature, we attract mostly positive people and situations that are a vibrational match. The opposite is also true. If our habitual thoughts and words are negative, what we attract is more negativity. That is also a vibrational match. Jesus declared this truth, "For those who have will receive more and they will have more than enough. But, as for those who don't have, even the little that they have will be taken away…" Matthew 13:12 (CEB)

For those with a positive vibration more positive situations and people will come into their lives to enhance and make even greater the good that they already have. When we bring what we call "good" into our life; and if we have a vibrational frequency that matches it, it will stay. If our vibrational frequency is of a negative nature, negativity and lack is what will be attracted. Therefore, even the little that we have will be taken away. When a person with a negative vibration stumbles onto what we might call blessings, the blessings will only stay if that person gets busy raising their level of vibration to a more positive one. Good stays with us by right of consciousness.

Those with a more negative vibration will attract more negativity, which will take away even what little goodness is in their lives. Positive vibrations cause increase. Negative vibrations cause decrease. In order to live the life of our dreams, we must take the necessary steps to raise our vibrational frequency to the level of our heart's desire. This is done by using the same methods described to raise our level of consciousness. The level of our consciousness determines our level of vibrational frequency.

Sometimes, we may feel like we can make ourselves deserving if we work really hard. We may think that somehow if we work 90 hours a week at our job, do volunteer work and make sacrifices for others we will be worthy of receiving a somewhat larger amount than we receive currently. We may think that there is a tipping point at which we can work hard enough or sacrifice enough to justify our existence. This is simply not true. The good news is that **there is no way to work yourself into worthiness**. It is freely given to everyone. Simply because you are born in the image of your Creator, you are worthy of good. If you were incapacitated and unable to do anything constructive for the rest of your life you are still worthy of all of the good of the universe just because of who you are. You are an expression of the Most High God. You were born worthy and deserving. What you choose to do with that worthiness will help determine the kind of life that you have. You will probably want to share your gifts by the work that you do but your work cannot make you more worthy and deserving. "The blessing of the Lord brings wealth without painful toil for it." Proverbs 10:22 (NIV)

When we embrace the heart's desire that God placed within each of us we create a vibrational match for it to come to us. Albert Einstein said, "Everything is energy and that's all there is. Match the frequency of the reality that you want and it is yours. There can be no other way. This is not philosophy. This is physics."

In order to live the life of our dreams, we do the necessary work to change our vibrational frequency. We do this by getting together with like-minded people, studying, praying, meditating and embracing the spiritual laws of success.

Perception

"We do not see things as **they** are; we see things as **we** are." The Talmud

The perception of lack comes from within our own mind. If we have a basic feeling that we are undeserving, we will see lack, scarcity, limitation and contraction in the world. When we know ourselves for who we really are, Precious Expressions of God, we know that we deserve good and we see the potential for abundance and opulence everywhere. We recognize that there is a world of substance just waiting to come into manifestation. As we evolve spiritually we begin to see things as they really are – unlimited. There is no limit to God's good. The substance from which all things are made is unlimited. As human beings we have difficulty grasping the concept of "unlimited". Our minds are more geared to understand a beginning and an ending to things. We would do well to open our minds to the vastness of the universe and simply accept that God's substance is unlimited and, as best we can, not allow our mind to place limits on it.

Learning to love yourself and see yourself the way God loves and sees you is a deep, lasting way of raising your level of vibration and attracting the life of your dreams. God sees you as whole and complete, lacking in nothing. It is only your perception of limitation that stops you from attracting and accepting into your life those things that God has prepared for you.

Affirmations

I am a precious child of God and I deserve all good.

I am perfect, whole and complete.

I love myself unconditionally.

CHAPTER II

Forgiveness is Not Optional

"To be wronged is nothing unless you continue to remember it."

Benjamin Franklin

"In order to live the opulent, abundant, joy-filled life that God intended, you must forgive everyone, of everything, all of the time, especially yourself, no exceptions."

Janie Kelley

Building the Foundation

Forgiveness is the second foundational principle of living a life of *freedom, joy and plenty*. When we have these two foundational principles in place (deservability and forgiveness) we can successfully move forward with the other spiritual principles which govern living the life of our dreams. Forgiveness frees up our energy and raises it to a clearer, higher vibration. It opens our hearts and causes a lightness of spirit that is unparalleled. Metaphorically speaking, forgiveness puts a song in our heart and a skip in our step.

Together, deservability and forgiveness create a "springboard" for the other spiritual principles of prosperity. The results that we get from forgiving ourselves and all others are worth the effort and the work involved. Complete forgiveness will bring peace of mind and body that, without it, would be impossible. Forgiveness is not optional.

Unforgiveness

Unforgiveness makes a mess of our lives and darkens our days! It blocks our physical and emotional health. It wrecks our relationships. It hinders our spiritual progress. When we are holding anyone in unforgiveness (ourselves included) it blocks the flow of prosperity, of all kinds, into our lives. It contracts our energy. Unforgiveness dams-up the flow of good in our lives; be it health, relationships, peace of mind or money.

When we hold unforgivnenss against any person, group of people, organization or situation it is like a "cosmic brick." Each cosmic brick is laid on another until a wall is formed. We may feel justified in the thoughts and actions that formed each one of these cosmic bricks. We may say to ourselves, "After all, under these circumstances, wouldn't anyone react this way? It was really terrible what she did! I have the right to be angry! She is not even sorry!" We may enlist other people in our drama in order to give even more credence to our story. In the end, the cosmic bricks still form the wall that blocks our good. It makes no difference if we feel justified. When we become hurt or angry with someone, don't we always feel justified? Of course we do! If we didn't, we would do it differently. Holding resentment in one's heart is like picking up a hot coal with the intention to throw it at the other person. Even if we hit them with it we will be the one most harmed.

By holding unforgiveness we are the ones who suffer. Much of the time the other person has no idea of the pain and misery that we are going through. Even if they did, the chances are slim that the whole thing is affecting them to the degree that it is affecting us.

The most recognized prayer in the Christian faith is The Lord's Prayer. In it we pray, "Forgive us our trespasses **as** we forgive those who trespass against us." By saying this, we are asking to be forgiven by the same measure that we forgive others. Do we really want that to be the case? Do we really want to receive forgiveness using the same "measuring stick" that we use in forgiving others? If we are quick to forgive, the answer is yes.

Everyone makes mistakes and needs the forgiveness of another at times. Sometimes, you are the forgiver and sometimes you are the "forgivee". Remember, what we give out is what we get back. You reap what we sow. Every major world religion teaches this Spiritual Truth. You receive forgiveness to the same degree that you give it.

In my life, I have been helped by remembering that, no matter what may offend me, at some point, as careful as I usually am, someone will be offended by my words, actions or omissions. I want to be forgiven by that person so it is up to me to give out that which I wish to get back. I remind myself that sometimes I am the forgiver and sometimes I am the forgivee.

Forgiveness Sets You Free

We forgive for ourselves. We forgive and release so that our mind is set free. We forgive and release so that there are no ill effects on our health, our work, our relationships or our money. We forgive and release so that the strong emotions do not keep us energetically tied to that person with invisible bonds of negativity. We forgive and release so that we can stay in the flow of the good that God has for us. It makes no difference if the person apologizes or not. It makes no difference if the person ever regrets the situation. It makes no difference if we think the person deserves forgiveness. We forgive to set our own selves free. What happens within the other person is between that person and God.

Forgiveness is **not** condoning abusive or destructive behavior. Forgiveness does not mean that you place a "stamp of approval" on the action or behavior. It is entirely possible to fully forgive **and** choose to remove yourself from the other person's presence. We should never place ourselves in harm's way in the name of forgiveness. If you have difficulty separating forgiveness from the approval of abusive or destructive behavior you might consider talking it over with someone in whom you trust. If you believe that you must accept an abusive person back into your life or you have not fully forgiven him or her, seek help resolving this issue. It is not okay to abuse another person and it is not okay to live in an abusive situation. Sometimes a strategy must be worked out prior to leaving for the safety of all concerned.

In my time of counseling with people, I have found that many people are not familiar with the concept of forgiving a person and at the same time releasing that person from their life. It seems to be a common misconception that to forgive a person means to fully accept that person back into one's life as if nothing happened even when it is not safe to do so. We are not meant to live our lives in any form of abuse, be it mental, physical, emotional, verbal or sexual. I highly recommend getting outside help if there is any doubt in your mind about such a situation. A trusted friend, counselor, minister or the local domestic abuse hotline can be very helpful to you in discerning the best course of action.

A daily practice of forgiving is necessary to keep you free of cosmic bricks that are blocking your prosperity. Before going to sleep each night ask God to show you if there is anyone that you need to forgive. Do you feel wronged by anyone? Have your feelings been hurt? Have you done something or failed to do something that needs forgiving? The larger offenses are easy to spot and will probably come to mind quickly. The tricky part comes in the small, seemingly insignificant incidents. Maybe it was an off-hand remark that someone made that did not set well with you. Maybe it was someone making a joke at your expense. Maybe it was a driver who would not let you merge into traffic on the freeway. Maybe it was the telling of a joke in your presence that you found offensive. Whatever it may be, these seemingly small offenses may not appear important at the time, and so, metaphysically speaking, you throw them over our shoulder and into your "cosmic backpack" and carry them around. You may not notice the weight at first because your cosmic backpack houses small offenses. When there are enough of these unforgiven incidents in your backpack it begins to weigh you down. You may find yourself irritable for no apparent reason. You may begin to feel sluggish and out of sorts and you really don't know why. If you did not do forgiveness work right away after the small offenses occurred then you will need to unload your backpack. Ask God to help you recall those incidents that need your attention and forgiveness. There may be incidents that you cannot recall, so set an intention to let go of every offense, including the ones that are outside your current memory. If you don't feel a need to recall each offense, you may want to say a prayer of forgiveness covering all of them.

When the forgiveness work is around something that we have done, we may need to do some clean-up work. This means we may need to go to a person (or people) and apologize. Depending on the offense, we may need to take some kind of action. It is important to our healing and to our forward movement to see that we take care of such things. It may be initially uncomfortable and difficult but the rewards will be worth it. The effort will be more than paid back in peace of mind and joyous, prosperous living. **Forgiveness is a necessary part of living a life you love.**

I don't believe that it is necessary to struggle to bring up every offense that we can squeeze out. We would do well just to let Spirit bring them gently into our awareness. We could open our hearts and minds and ask God to show us, in a gentle way, what we need to forgive at any moment in time. Whatever we need to address will come up to be healed in perfect timing. There is no need to struggle. It is, however, most important to do this work daily or at least regularly. It is also beneficial to take a few hours, half a day or a full day, at regular intervals, to go deep within and allow God to reveal any hidden work that needs to be done. This kind of practice has a cleansing affect that will pay off in the long run with a lighter, easier way of living. There may be people or incidents for which we have done forgiveness work to the extent that we were capable at the time. Possibly deeper forgiveness work is necessary to release the offense completely. By doing this longer practice every 3-6 months, we help keep ourselves in the flow of God's good. A good, all-inclusive prayer/affirmation is one by Catherine Ponder.

"All that offends me, I forgive

All persons, all things, I forgive completely.

Within and without, I forgive.

Myself and all others I forgive.

Especially myself, I forgive."

This prayer is like a mental broom that sweeps through our minds and gets rid of the "cobwebs of unforgiveness" that may be too small to see. When we have a sincere desire and have set an intention to release all unforgiveness from our lives The Creator honors that and helps us to sweep our minds clean.

Spiritual Fitness

Forgiveness is an ongoing exercise and must be done regularly. You cannot expect to do it once and for all or only occasionally and expect optimum results. You would not work out at the gym once a month and expect your body to get into shape and stay in shape. You would not expect to work with a trainer every day for two weeks and stop then blame your trainer because the benefits did not last. Forgiveness work is very similar. It must be done daily or at least regularly for the rest of your life if you expect ongoing results. It is one of the practices which helps keep you spiritually fit.

The only way that there is nothing to forgive is when you have released ALL judgment. When you judge **nothing**, there is nothing to forgive.

Forgiveness and Health

Besides the spiritual benefits of forgiveness, there are proven benefits for the mind and body as well. According to research done by staff members at a world famous clinic some of the benefits of forgiveness are; healthier relationships, greater spiritual and psychological well-being, less anxiety, less stress, less hostility, regulated blood pressure, strengthened immune system, fewer symptoms of depression, lower risk of alcohol and substance abuse and lower risk of physical illness.

These are just some of the practical reasons to make forgiveness work a priority your life. The benefits of a regular forgiveness practice have a far reaching effect on the quality of your life. I am sure that there are benefits that have not yet been discovered.

Free-Floating Anger

There is a term called "free-floating anger." This term refers to feelings of anger that are always just below the surface of one's emotions just waiting to attach themselves to something. Free-floating anger is a feeling that affects almost every part of a person's life when it is present. Some, if not all, of this unidentified anger has to do with unforgiveness and unresolved issues in the person's life. This free-floating anger will surface over some of the smallest offenses and show up as the person over-reacting to a situation. Forgiveness work is usually very beneficial in releasing the free-floating anger issues. The deeper and more long-term the issues, the more likely help will be needed.

If you find that you react with anger to most situations in your life that do not go according to your plan or expectation, if anger is a frequent response on your part or if your anger is often disproportionate to the circumstances, you may want to look at this issue of free-floating anger. Professional help may be needed.

Judge with Right Judgment

When we feel the need to forgive a person or situation, it is because a judgment has taken place. We have made a judgment that a person has done something that they should not have done or omitted doing something that they should have done. We may judge a situation as being unfair or just not right.

Jesus said, "Do not judge by appearances but judge with right judgment." John 7:24 (NRSV) Great advice! But, what is right judgment? I believe that the only "right judgment" would come from Spirit because our Creator sees the whole picture and knows **all** of the facts. As human beings, **we never will know all of the facts**. We may think that we know all of the facts about a person or a given situation; we may think that we see the big picture but we do not. Humans are capable of seeing only a very small fraction of the whole picture. Even if we could know all of the facts and see the big picture, the information is still processed through the filters of our minds. These filters are made up of all of our experiences and the information that we have taken in up to that point. So, having all of the facts or seeing the big picture would still not be enough to judge with right judgment because our filters would distort facts based on our own limited and/or skewed perceptions.

Some time ago, I was ruminating over an incident that happened to me that I believed was unfair. I believed that unrealistic expectations had been placed on me by a person I love, admire and trust. I felt hurt and angry about it. We had cross words over it and I was still in the place of thinking I was right. I had not yet gotten to the point of releasing it to God. I guess that I wanted to wallow in it a little longer. I was in the middle of all of that when I was suddenly stopped by "the voice of God." It was not an audible voice but it was unmistakable. I have heard this "voice" enough times that I instantly got the message. One of the ways that God speaks to me is through thoughts that are not my own. These thoughts have a distinctive way of coming to me and have a "sound" about them. The words do not come like we would pronounce words in a row to convey a thought. In an instant, I have a knowing and then the message comes later in the form of words. The messages are always in the fewest words possible and come straight to the point. While I was still upset, the message came to me, "**You're never going to know all the facts.**" It had my attention because I recognized the voice. Basically, God was telling me that there was more to the story than I knew and that I would never know it all. The message I got was, "Let it go!" That was my signal to stop, forgive, release my anger and return to my center where peace and harmony abide. I also knew in an instant that the message not only applied to this particular situation but it also applied to every other situation that I would ever encounter, or had ever encountered, both personally and globally. I am never going to know all of the facts about any given situation or any person, even if I think I do. That message has made a profound difference in my life. Since then when I encounter situations and people, on any level, I am aware that I will never know all of the facts and I am not as likely to make a judgment about the situation or person. I am also aware that none of us will ever know all of the facts about any given situation or person, even if we think that we do.

"Do not judge by appearances but judge with right judgment." It is only if we could get to the place of judging in the same way that God does (which is not judging at all) will we be able to judge with right judgment. When we get to the place of non-judgment there will be nothing to forgive because we have judged nothing as wrong or defective. If we have not judged "by appearances" in the first place we are relieved of the responsibility of forgiving. This is a worthy goal on which to fix our aim.

Discernment is different from judging. Judging is criticizing and making wrong. Discernment is when we use wisdom in deciding whether a person or situation is in our best interest or the best interest of a certain situation.

Until we get to the place of non-judgment, we will continue our practice of forgiving everyone, of everything, all of the time, including ourselves, no exceptions.

Checks and Balances

For every seeming challenge or difficulty that we encounter in our lives there is potentially a gift of equal proportion. There is a perfect system of checks and balances in the universe. Whenever we encounter a difficult experience in life, there comes with it the potential for a beautiful gift of equal proportion. The gift may be disguised to the point that we do not recognize it as a gift, but it is given to us never the less. Sometimes our gift of equal proportion may come from a completely different area or source. Sometimes we may need to s-t-r-e-t-c-h our minds far beyond what we have ever done in order to recognize the gift. When we have those people and situations in our lives where we need to forgive, we may ask our self or God, "Why is this happening to me?" It may seem terribly unfair and unjust. It may be difficult to see a gift in it at first but, it is very important to stay open and aware until the gift reveals itself.

In the early nineties I attended continuing education classes at Unity Village, the headquarters of the Unity Movement. It is located near Kansas City, Missouri and houses Silent Unity (a 24-hour prayer line), Unity Seminary, Unity Retreats, Spiritual Education and Enrichment classes as well as the Unity Administrative Staff. Each class was two hours a day for one week with a total of ten hours per class. These classes are a pre-requisite for applying to Unity Seminary and other leadership roles within the Unity Movement. I signed up for three required classes and one elective. The elective class was titled simply, *"Forgiveness"* taught by Reverend Don Jennings. I thought that I had come a long way in the area of forgiveness and this class would be easy. I thought to myself, "Of course I know how to forgive. My life has given me lots of opportunities to practice forgiveness. Besides, there is no such thing as too much forgiveness." So, I signed up. I did not have a clue that this class would be a defining moment in my life.

Have you ever had those times when you moved forward on a decision based on what you thought you knew and God had a much grander plan in mind? This was one of those times. I thought I was taking this elective class which would give me 10 more credits toward my certificate and that it would be a breeze.

The class began with Rev. Jennings making the statement, "All forgiveness is self-forgiveness." I thought, "What?" Then a hundred things went through my mind in about 18 seconds. You know how you do when your mind wants to reject an idea that is foreign to it. Then I thought things like, "How can all forgiveness be self-forgiveness? What about when someone does something intentionally mean to me? What is this instructor talking about? Why did I sign up for this class anyway? Is it too late to withdraw?"

For reasons, unknown to me at the time, I did not drop the class. I was probably intrigued and wanted to know how the instructor would back up such a statement. As the week progressed, Rev. Jennings developed the idea into a form that I could at least begin to understand. It would take much concentration on my part. It took much more time, than that one week, for me to really grasp the concept that he presented. This teaching was so far outside of conventional wisdom that I had no frame of reference in which to place it so that I could process it. Conventional wisdom had taught me, "To err is human. To forgive, divine." After all, when I forgive someone else when they "err", am I not being "divine"? Isn't it wonderful of me to forgive that other person no matter how wrong they were? Didn't forgiving them make me godly? I thought I was doing them a favor! That was my level of consciousness at that time. Now this well respected minister and instructor was telling me that I am only forgiving myself.

You know how we get whatever teaching we need whenever we need it and are ready for it? What I got from his teaching was this:

If I am offended by another person, I have made a judgment about what that person should or should not have done. I then make a choice to forgive that person only to realize that life mirrors back to me what is within me. If life mirrors back to me that which is within me then the potential for the same offense was first in me (whether or not I have ever acted on it). I then forgive myself for having this potential offense within me or having committed this offense. That is how I understand the statement, "All forgiveness is self-forgiveness."

Just as I thought that I was about to get it, the Rev. Jennings dropped another bombshell on the last day of class. He said, "When we release all judgment there is nothing to forgive. Until we release all judgment, we can continue to forgive ourselves for having made a judgment in the first place. All forgiveness is self-forgiveness." Again I thought, "Huh! What is he talking about? Why did I sign up for this class?" Once again, I had no frame of reference to take this in. Now he is telling me that I should move toward the place of non-judgment where there is nothing to forgive! Non-judgment means seeing people and situations as neither good nor bad.

How could I possibly do that? Is it even possible for a human being to get to the place of non-judgment? Well, more than twenty years later, I am still working on that last question. Jesus said, "Love your enemies." What happens when we love our enemies? We have no more enemies. There is nothing left to judge.

This teaching has turned out to be one of the most profound of my life and one of the most freeing! Reverend Don Jennings turned out to be one of the most important teachers of my life. That is the one and only class I ever took from him. The opportunity never presented itself again. He was in my life for a reason and a short season.

During that same week, in a different class, an exercise was given. We were instructed to think of the worst thing that had ever happened to us in our entire lives. At first I had the inclination to pick something less than the worst thing. You know how your mind sometimes doesn't want to recall a difficult period in your life, especially if you feel like you have dealt with it and placed it in a neat package in a dark corner of your mind. Anyway, who would know? I could pick a lesser thing and maybe I would not become so emotional about it. After all, I was in this class with people whom I had never met before this week. I did all of the rationalizing that I could think of and, for whatever reason, I allowed myself to dredge-up the very hardest and worst part in my entire life (up to that point), my twenty-year marriage and the divorce which ended it.

The instructor said, "Now take this 'worst thing of your life' and write about it. Take twenty minutes and write everything you can think of about that event or situation. Make it as detailed as possible. Write what happened, what you were feeling, any conversation which is relevant and even what you were wearing if it seems important. Allow yourself to write about whatever comes up." I thought that I had dealt with that period of my life and yet layers of ugliness started to pour out of me. The thought came to me that I had already had a lot of counseling and done much processing around this very dark chapter of my life and I thought the pain and resentment were over once and for all. As I wrote, fear gripped my throat and tears stung my eyes as I started to cry. I felt some of the same gut-wrenching feelings I had felt when it was all happening. I wasn't just writing **about** the story, I found myself **in** the story once again. I was not just remembering it, I was reliving it. Lots of very emotionally charged thoughts were coming out and onto the paper. I allowed myself to feel the feelings even in a room full of strangers. Somehow their presence no longer mattered to me. It all came pouring out. Then the time was up.

Our instructor said, "Now on a separate sheet of paper, write the gifts that you received from the worst thing that has ever happened to you." I did not see that coming! Gifts? He must be kidding? Is he serious? How could there be gifts? It changed the course of my whole life! Wait, that's it! It changed the course of my whole life. That was the first gift that I recognized. I was starting to get it. I was in a devastatingly unhappy and terribly abusive marriage until the abuse went too far. Why wouldn't I want something to change the course of my life? What a gift! And then the other gifts started pouring out of me. It came to me that I had the gift of much better self-esteem. As a result of the divorce, I took the time to really get to know myself and to nurture myself. I no longer lived in a situation in which, no matter how hard I tried, I was "not enough". Had I still been in that marriage, my self-esteem would have only gotten much worse. I now know that I am a precious child of God and I deserve all good. **I am enough!** I also received the gift of knowing that I can stand on my own and make my way in the world. I had the opportunity to own and operate two businesses, simultaneously, for twenty-three years and to learn so many valuable lessons from having done that. Because I had my businesses, I met many interesting people and had many world experiences that I would not have otherwise known. I had opportunities to travel that never would have come to me had I still been in that very restrictive marriage. I was able to take advantage of certain educational opportunities because I was single. The world opened up to me in new and exciting ways that I had never even imagined. I, most likely, would not even have been at Unity Village at that very moment taking that very insightful class if I had not gone through that marriage and divorce. It took all that happened in my life to get me to the present time! When I completed the writing I knew that I had just begun to recognize the gifts that came as a result of that marriage and divorce. Today, I bless all the experiences that have made up my life. I know that, to get to where I am today, I could have come no other way.

I will say that the sting of the divorce had not completely left me at the time of that writing exercise but today I wish him well and pray that he would have all of the good things that life has to offer him. I have conversed with him when the situation called for it and with only positive emotions.

I now believe that we all do the best that we can given the amount of information and experience that we have at the time. I am in no way condoning or making excuses for abusive and destructive behavior.

We must wipe the slate clean, so to speak, and keep it clean by forgiving everyone, of everything, all of the time, especially ourselves, no exceptions. By staying in a state of being "forgiven-up", we open wide the floodgates of heaven and clear the decks to receive our good!

Affirmations

I forgive everyone, of everything, all of the time, especially myself, no exceptions.

I allow myself to feel the freedom that comes with forgiveness.

I live in a state of non-judgment.

Chapter III

Attitude of Gratitude

"If the only prayer you ever pray is 'Thank You' that will suffice."

Meister Eckhart

"When we place our focus on gratitude, a miracle happens. We find even more in our lives for which to be grateful."

Janie Kelley

Choice

Gratitude is a choice. We have a choice whether we will live our lives in a state of general gratitude or we can choose a different state of mind. It is choosing to live life with the proverbial glass half-empty or the glass half-full. We each have a choice and we make that choice in every moment of our lives. At any given moment there are people and situations for which we can be grateful and there are things that our mind can find to play the "Ain't It Awful" game. Isn't it wonderful that we get to choose!

That does not mean that difficult situations will not happen. There will be challenges in life. Jesus said it very well, "In the world you will have tribulation but be of good cheer for I have overcome the world." John 16:33 (NKJV) Two things that we know from this scripture and from life experience; we will face challenges and **for every problem there is a solution**.

We can take the same set of circumstances and see the situation with a positive attitude or see it from a negative standpoint. Even in the most difficult of circumstances, such as the loss of a loved one, we can have the faith that the pain will lessen over time and we are never alone in it. God is always with/ within us. We always have everything we need to get to a place of peace.

There is a song by Roger Miller that contains these lines, "Some people walk in the rain, others just get wet." Isn't that a great example! What do you think is the difference? Attitude! Two people may have the same set of circumstances and one "walks in the rain" while the other "just gets wet." It is all in our attitude and perception of the event.

A person may look out on a snowy day and say "What a miserable day! I guess I will just have to stay in". Another person may look out at the same snowy day and say, "What a great day! Get out the skis!" In and of itself, it is neither a miserable day nor a great day. It is simply a snowy day; that is all. It is perception that makes the difference. Perception plays a powerful role in our lives!

There is a difference in being thankful *for* a set of circumstances and being thankful *in* a set of circumstances. It is good to be thankful for a person or situation. It is even better to have an overarching thankfulness about life. This means that you have made up your mind, in advance, to look for ways to be positive and to be grateful, no matter what. You have made a commitment to look for the good in situations, circumstances and people, including yourself. Making up your mind, in advance, is the key to an overarching attitude of gratitude. If you move into each day without having made this choice in advance, there will be opportunities at every turn to have negative self-talk, to make negative judgments and have negative experiences. These opportunities may come in the form of the news, your child's behavior, conversations at work, high prices, the way other people behave in traffic, uncomfortable weather, and the list is endless. Life affords you many opportunities to choose an attitude of gratitude, or not. The choice is yours. You bring about what you think about.

The Bible says, "Rejoice evermore. Pray without ceasing. *In* everything give thanks; for this is the will of God…" I Thessalonians 5:16-18 (KJV) It does not say *for* everything give thanks. We do not have to be thankful for the circumstances in life when we are experiencing difficulty. We can, however, have an attitude of gratitude *in* the circumstances. The difference is that, with a commitment to an attitude of gratitude, you can find something for which to be grateful no matter what circumstance; even if it is only the knowledge that everything is temporary and, in time, it will pass. You have the freedom to choose your attitude.

Are you walking in the rain or just getting wet? It is all in the attitude and perception. If you are walking in the rain you may really love that activity. However, it may also be that you have come to a place in life where you see the advantage of making the best of what is, living in the moment and seeing the beauty of it.

When we make up our minds in advance to look at the world from a positive vantage point, it has an effect on everything that we encounter. *A Course in Miracles* teaches, *"There is always another way of looking at this."* I have found this to be true in my own life.

There will be times in life that we can change our circumstances if we so choose. We are much more powerful than most of us realize. And there will be times over which we have little or no control of the situation or the outcome. Peace comes when we make the choice to change what we can and to accept that for which we have no apparent control. Just as the very popular Serenity Prayer states:

God, grant me the serenity

To accept the things I cannot change,

The courage to change the things I can,

And the wisdom to know the difference.

Reinhold Niebuhr

We co-create with God for our lives! We are much more powerful than most of us allow ourselves to recognize!

The Law of Mind Action

"You are creating your life either by design or default." Mary Morrissey

Your mind is creating your life! You are either creating it on purpose by consciously choosing your thoughts or you are creating it based on old thought patterns that may have been replaying for years. Either way, your mind is creating your life.

- Thoughts held in mind produce after their kind.
- What you give your attention to grows stronger in your life.
- What you focus on expands.
- You bring about what you think about.
- As a person thinks, so is that person.

However it is stated, the message is the same, your thoughts help create your life. God gives you the all of the "raw material" needed with which to create the life of your dreams. You have intelligence, strength, imagination, will, faith, understanding, love, power and wisdom, just to name a few of your innate faculties. God also places opportunities in your life to help you along your way. At times, these opportunities are disguised as problems. The thoughts that you choose to think are like seeds in the fertile soil of your mind. Although it may not seem like it at times, we get to choose which "thought seeds" we plant.

A belief system is simply made up of habitual thoughts that we have decided, on some level, are true. Our habitual thoughts create our belief system and our belief system affects our overall attitude about life in general. Much of our belief system was created from thoughts passed to us when we were very young. Many of them came to us so long ago that we can't even remember where they originated. Many of our deepest held spiritual beliefs originated with someone else. We have accepted many of our beliefs because someone that we respected told us that they were true. Examine your beliefs. "Test everything". If a belief does not serve to make a better life we would do well to change it. All we need to do to change a belief is to change our thoughts around that particular belief. If a series of thoughts created this belief then a series of different thoughts will create a different belief. *A way we know that a particular belief is valid and true is that, ultimately, it brings joy and/or peace of mind.*

For instance, I picked up the belief, somewhere, that certain reactions are inevitable when a specific event or situation occurs. Some of these reactions are:

- If someone cuts me off in traffic; I become angry
- If a loved one is late getting home; I become worried and anxious
- If a relationship ends; I become sad and depressed.
- If I receive a gift; I feel happy
- If a situation does not go the way I want; I become irritated or angry

The truth is that none of these reactions are automatic. They are reactions we have learned. We have a choice to either let them be a part of our life, or not. If these reactions no longer work for us, for whatever reason, we would do well to let them go and, in the resulting vacuum, fill the space with something beneficial.

One day, in heavy Houston, Texas traffic, I became angry with another driver when the thought occurred to me, "I have a choice about this." I decided to send blessings to the other driver and let it go. It worked better than I could have even imagined. I not only let go of the situation on that day, but my attitude about other drivers on the road began to change. One day, when a person's driving forced me to the shoulder of the road instead of becoming angry I burst into spontaneous laughter. I didn't understand it but it certainly felt better than being irritated or angry. No one was hurt. Nothing was damaged. The laughter was spontaneous and a positive way of releasing tension and letting go of the incident. Since that time my reaction to most driving incidents is laughter. With the laughter I can easily release the situation. What a gift! God really does have a sense of humor!

The average person thinks tens of thousands of thoughts a day and more than ninety per cent of those thoughts are repeated thoughts from the past. If we want to live the life of our dreams, and we are not currently doing that, we must start by changing our thoughts. If we continue to have the same thoughts that we had in the past, we will continue to have the same results. *If nothing changes, nothing changes.*

If you are in an attitude that you do not like and this attitude is not producing the results that you want, set about to change your thoughts thus changing your attitude. In order to cultivate an attitude of gratitude within yourself where one does not exist, thoughts must be changed. *Change your thoughts, change your life.* This may seem simplistic but many of the most profound, life-changing teachings are simple in nature. If you find that you are living in a state other than gratitude, and you wish to change it, start by making a conscious decision to be thankful for specific people and circumstances. Make it a point to see the good in your life. If your negative attitude has taken you down to a level where it is difficult for you to see good in much of anything, start by looking at the simple things in life. For instance, there was enough cereal and milk for breakfast, there was plenty of hot water for your shower, your car started easily so that you could go to work, your dog greeted you with a wagging tail, etc. Use this affirmation daily, "Look for the good." Make it your mantra; "Look for the good, look for the good, look for the good".

You may not believe that you can take control of your thoughts, but some of the most brilliant minds that have ever lived on our planet tell us that it not only can be done but must be done to bring about lasting change of any kind. We must gain control of our thoughts and consequently our attitude.

Choose Your Own Way

No matter what the situation, we have a choice about the attitude we will form around it. We may not be able to change the current set of circumstances but we have the ability to choose the thoughts we have regarding it.

An extreme example is in the book, *Man's Search for Meaning*, the author, Viktor Frankl, was an Austrian psychiatrist who, in 1942, was taken prisoner along with his wife and parents. They were separated from each other and sent to different concentration camps. He suffered atrocities that most of us, will never have to face. Ultimately, he lost every member of his family.

He wrote, "We who lived in the concentration camps can remember the men who walked through the huts comforting others; giving away their last piece of bread. They may have been few in number, but they offer sufficient proof that everything can be taken from a man but one thing; the last of the human freedoms – to choose one's attitude in any given set of circumstances; to choose one's own way."

Granted this is an extreme example and most of us have never, and will never, be faced with such unspeakable horror as a concentration camp. We can look at the life of Viktor Frankl, and the prisoners that he wrote about, and know that if it was possible for them to gain control of their own thoughts and attitudes, it is certainly possible for us.

We have the ability to choose the nature of our thoughts. We can choose, in advance, how we are going to approach life in general. Knowing that we have a choice, we may want to ask ourselves this question, "Do the thoughts that I am thinking have benefit? Do they serve to bring me joy or peace of mind?" We, alone, control our own thoughts. No matter what the behavior, no matter what the circumstance, we have the power to choose our thoughts and our attitude.

As Louise Hay says, "You are the only thinker in your mind." We may think that others make us think certain thoughts or make us act and react in certain ways but the truth is this; it is our own choice. We may *allow* a person to have a measure of control over our mind but they can only control our mind with our permission. We would do well to pay attention to our thoughts during the day and see what kinds of habitual thoughts are present in our minds.

There is a story about a group of young monks who were being trained in the ways of that particular sect of Buddhism. The older monk who was doing the training was very wise indeed. He taught the monks that if they gained control of their thoughts, such a skill would certainly help them to attain enlightenment. He said, "You must first know what thoughts you are thinking so that you can continue with the ones that lead you to enlightenment and release the ones that do not." He went on to tell them that most of their thoughts were habitual and had been around in their minds for so many years that they did not even know that they were thinking those particular thoughts. In order to help the young monks identify their thoughts he used this exercise. At random times of the day he would ring a bell. At the sound of the bell the young monks were to stop whatever they were doing and bring to mind their last thought. By identifying the thought, the monks could then make a conscious choice about whether the thought was a beneficial one and, therefore, one that they wanted to cultivate. If it was not one that was beneficial, they could then make a conscious decision to release it and replace it with a more enlightened thought.

I have done this exercise on my own and, each time I do, it is quite interesting to recall my thoughts when the timer goes off. I set a timer without looking at it to see the amount of time that was set. I place the timer in my pocket and go about whatever I was doing. After I had practiced this exercise several times I found that I began to do it somewhat spontaneously. I, periodically, came to the awareness of my last thought without the use of a timer. At that point, I could choose to release it from my thought life or I could embrace it. Try it. It can be a very freeing experience. A word of advice; set your device on a soft setting so that you are not startled when it rings. Being startled will likely cause you to forget your most recent thought and remembering it is the point of the exercise.

There was a time in my life when I did not know that I had a choice about my thoughts and attitude. I didn't know that I had choices about much in my life. I thought that I had to get up each morning, face the day, take whatever life threw at me and deal with it the best way that I knew how, go to bed, get up and do the same thing the next day. It is no wonder that, over the years, I became depressed to the point of suicide. With a belief system that included such a feeling of helplessness and victimhood, how could I possibly think that my life would ever be any better? I thought that certain attitudes just naturally sprang up around certain sets of circumstances and certain types of people. I thought that there were automatic responses attached to each situation. If things went the way that I thought that they should, my attitude was good. If circumstances were less than favorable for me, my attitude was not so good and if things went really badly my attitude was "the pits!" If people behaved in a way that I thought was acceptable, my attitude was good. If people did not behave the way that I thought they should, my attitude was…well, you get the picture. "After all", I thought, "wouldn't anyone react this way under these circumstances?" I felt like I could reinforce and justify my attitude by drawing others into my story. The more people I could get to agree with me, the more positive I was that I was right. *A Course in Miracles* states, "Would you rather be right or happy?" Frankly, back then in my terribly unenlightened, depressed state I would rather have been right than happy. In my family of origin being right was of paramount importance and I had carried on that tradition.

Many years ago, I was in my therapist's office and I was in my usual victim stance. I was telling her some story about how terribly I had been treated by someone. I really don't remember my story exactly and the facts of the story are unimportant. When I finally took a breath, she said, "You have a choice about this." I said, "You don't understand…,"

and then I went into telling my story again about how I had been victimized. She waited until I came up for air and said, "You have a choice about this." Now she was really starting to get on my nerves! Couldn't she see that I had no choice and that I was doing the only thing that could be done under the circumstances? I argued with her. She continued to say, "You have a choice about this." Now I was really angry! I thought, "I am paying her to tell me this nonsense! Whose side is she on, anyway?" She went on to explain some of my possible choices as she could see them. Then she said the clincher, "Everything in life is a choice with the possible exception of when you die. You may not be able to change a given situation but you have a choice about how you react to it and your attitude toward it." Well then, I'd had it! I stopped arguing with her only because I was stumped. I had never heard of such a thing! I left her office confused, baffled and most of all, angry with her. I went through the whole gamut of thoughts, "That is easy for her to say in her safe, secure, protected little world. What does she know about real life, anyway? Maybe if I explain to her one more time, she will understand." After a few days of resisting her words, I gave up and started to try to understand what she was saying to me. The concept was so foreign to me that I had to create a whole new paradigm in my mind just to begin to understand it. Nothing in my life, up to that point, had prepared me for this totally new way of approaching life. Then I started to get it. I *do* have choices. Maybe I *can* control how I respond to it. Maybe I *can* control my attitude. Opening my mind to that concept turned out to be one of the defining moments in my life. It was and is a beautiful freedom.

It took a while for me to comprehend it. It simply never occurred to me that I had a choice about much of anything in life beyond what to wear or cook for dinner. For years I had reacted in ways that I thought I was supposed to under the given set of circumstances. It took some time before I really got it that I have a choice about my thoughts, my attitude and most everything else in my life. Today I believe that everything in my life involves choice. It may appear that I am not consciously choosing the set of circumstances but I always have a choice about my attitude concerning it. Today I know that my thoughts and my attitudes are my personal responsibility. It is one of my delights in life to help another person come into these realities of choice just as my therapist did for me. I now know that I co-create my life with God through my thoughts, words and actions. I believe that God gives me all of the raw material and all of the advantages that I will ever need. The rest is up to me. Knowing that everything in my life involves choice has significantly changed my life in a most positive way.

Prayer, Attitude and Choice

Just before going to seminary, my two dogs and I, lived on an acre of property in a large, two-story house. My house had three bedrooms, three bathrooms, and a huge detached garage with a workshop, a swimming pool and many large, old pecan trees. At that point, I had lived there about twenty-six years. At this same time, after years of taking preparatory classes and meeting the requirements, I was accepted into Unity Seminary. I knew long before I even applied to school that I wanted to live on the grounds at Unity Village where the seminary was located. I wanted to be in the heart of Unity and be available to all that was offered during the time that I was in school. I wanted to be able to step outside my door and walk the beautiful, fragrant, manicured grounds, walk to the Peace Chapel and sit in meditation, pray with people who called Silent Unity for prayer, walk the labyrinth, visit the wonderful, metaphysical library that I love so much and take advantage of many of the other events and opportunities at Unity Village. I knew that I was to live in the vibrational energy of this piece of earth that had been bathed in prayer for more than 100 years. To do that meant that I would live in student housing. This involved living in a 100+ year-old house with five other people. Six people living in one house with two bathrooms and one very small kitchen. From all outward signs, this set up had the potential of being a challenge, to say the least.

Even before I knew that I had been accepted into seminary, I started praying for the perfect house on grounds, the perfect room (each room was different) and the perfect housemates. When any negative thought crept into my mind that my house, my room or my housemates might be anything other than perfect, I would begin praying and affirming the best for myself. I set my attitude on the positive and declared in my heart-of-hearts that my experience there was going to be wonderful! My intention and my attitude were set!

God had placed within me a heart's desire to live on the grounds at Unity Village. I acted on that heart's desire by praying, affirming and adjusting my attitude to be open to receive the gift.

It turned out that I was assigned to the house called "The Annex". I believe that it was originally built to accommodate people who came to stay at Unity Village for extended periods of time; maybe a month or more. There is also student housing called, "The Hotel" that was built for shorter stays and had smaller rooms. It turned out that I was assigned an upstairs room (I really enjoy an upstairs bedroom) that had three closets. Three closets! This was a dream come true! In my room were two sets of windows. One set of windows overlooked the beautiful, green and well-manicured golf course. When the weather was right, I would open my windows for fresh air and sometimes the conversations of the golfers came in clearly. Interesting conversations happen on a golf course! From the other set of windows I could see The Unity Tower which is a defining landmark of Unity Village that can be seen from a distance as one approaches "The Village." It is beautiful and stately. It stands for faith and hope in the minds of many of us. From these windows, in the evenings, I could see deer and many small animals as they came out for night feedings. I had the most wonderful housemates! I could not have done better if I had hand-picked them. After having three bathrooms to myself in my home, I shared a small bathroom with two other women. With a morning schedule that the three of us agreed upon, I never found it to be a real problem. Six of us shared a kitchen that was about 10x12. My house, my room, my housemates and our gatherings around the kitchen table are some of the most precious memories of my time in seminary. I loved my teachers and I loved my classes. I loved my classmates. I loved my time in that wonderful, old house. I made up my mind, in advance, that my experience was going to be great and it exceeded anything that I allowed myself to expect.

We have the ability to make up our minds in advance what attitude we will take on any subject or about any person. Why not pick a good one?

Attitude about Money

If we are to welcome money into our lives, we must treat it with gratitude and respect. We would do well to take a good look at how we treat our physical money. Do we treat it with respect or do we crumple and crush it into our pocket, purse or wallet? This would include our checks, debit cards, credit cards, gift cards and anything that represents money. Do we have money lying around in many places? Do we balance our checkbook? Do we keep a spending record so that we know where our money is going? Treat your money well. Respect your money. It shows the universe that you mean business!

Money represents energy. Money is energy. Quantum physicists have discovered that we change the probable structure of an object by merely placing our attention on it. With positive energy, we enhance the object to which we give our attention. With negative energy, we have the opposite effect on the object. How we treat our money is very important in attracting more money to us.

Clean out and organize your wallet and/or purse. File or throw away old receipts, business cards and papers. Once it is clean and organized, keep it clean. Place your money neatly in your wallet all bills facing the same direction. Do the same with any checks, credit cards, debit cards and gift cards that you have. This may seem a little silly at first but keep an open mind. As already established, money is energy. We are energy. We imbue the things we touch with our energy. When we handle our money without respect the energy is contracted. When we handle it with appreciation and respect for what it can do to help us to live the life of our dreams, we imbue it with expanding energy.

Keep a spending record. This is not a budget. It is simply a record of the amount of money that you spent, where you spent it and the date. This is another way of showing respect for your money. When you buy something, write it down on a small pad that you keep with you. By doing this you are telling the universe that you are a good manager of a smaller amount and you will be made manager over more. The spending record helps you to know where your money is going. I have found that a pocket-size daily appointment book works really well. The day's date is already done for you and makes jotting down the amount and where it was spent much quicker than a plain note pad where you must write in the date also.

Have you ever gone to the bank or ATM, withdrawn $100, put it in your wallet and after a short period of time, it was gone? You may have thought or said, "What happened to the hundred dollars I withdrew?" The well-kept spending record will eliminate that question and show the universe that you can be trusted to handle even more money.

It is the same with your checking account. By keeping your checking account balance up to date you are showing yet another way that you respect the money with which you have been entrusted. Don't forget to keep receipts from the use of your debit card and deduct those, as well. The checkbook is also a good record for knowing where your money is going.

Even if you are skeptical of any of the suggestions I have given, remember that I asked you to suspend all that you thought that you knew about life and money until you have read this entire book and have done all of the required work. If your habits and actions have not worked well for you in the past, what do you have to lose? What if there is really something to all of this and you miss it!

Prayer

"More things are wrought by prayer than the world dreams of." Alfred Lord Tennyson Prayer in some form is practiced and taught by all of the major world religions. Throughout recorded history, there have been accounts of prayer. Prayer is not to change the mind of a capricious God, but to align our own minds with the God-Mind.

We are not praying to inform God of anything. Do you think that you are going to surprise The Omniscient with some brand new information? Praying is not to ask God for something that God knew nothing about until you made the information available. God knows what you need before you ever ask. The answers to your prayers are already present in Spirit anyway. You need only align your mind with the Mind of Spirit and in the fullness of time the prayer is answered. Sometimes your prayers are answered in a different way than you expect, so keep your heart and mind open to recognize the answer when it comes.

There is no wrong way to pray. We pray from our own level of consciousness. When we were children we prayed prayers such as:

"God is great; God is good.

Let us thank Him for our food.

By His hand we are fed.

Give us now our daily bread.

Amen."

At that time, we prayed from a child's level of consciousness. As time goes by, we may become more adept at expressing ourselves, but we would do well to continue to come from a place of simplicity. God is not looking to be impressed by our eloquent words. God looks upon our hearts. It is that simple. We continue to pray from our level of consciousness and that level changes over time as we grow spiritually. Again I say there is no wrong way to pray. We simply pray however it feels best. Some might feel more comfortable addressing The Universal Power in a more formal manner such as Dear God or Almighty God and then continue the prayer in more formal language. Still others may feel that a less formal approach is more appealing. I have a good friend who addresses God as "My Friend and Heavenly Parent" and sometimes simply, "My Friend". We pray best from our level of consciousness and from our level of comfort.

God knows the desires of your heart. After all, God placed them there.

The Power of the Spoken Word

When we get clear in our own minds, we speak the words and write the words that send a clear message to the Universe. Speak your prayers aloud either alone or with other people of like consciousness. Several powerful things happen when a prayer is spoken audibly. The mental intention, as well as, the vibration of the sound of the words is picked up by every cell in your body. We used to believe that the mind was in the brain and the brain did the thinking. Now, research shows that every living cell of the body is a thinking organism and is sensitive to intention and sound vibrations. Also, the sound sends out a vibrational frequency that moves out and finds its perfect match. That perfect vibrational match is the answer to the prayer. Prayers spoken aloud with emotion have added power.

Remember, *"Everything is energy and that is all there is to it. Match the frequency of the reality that you want and you cannot help but get that reality. This is not philosophy. This is physics."* (Albert Einstein) In positive prayer, you "match the frequency of the reality you want".

The Power of the Written Word

There is power in written prayer that is definite. The written prayer can be read and reread to impress upon the mind what is being declared. One purpose of prayer is to adjust our own thinking. Our prayers are already answered before we speak them, write them or even think them. A very enriching practice is to keep a prayer journal. If you already keep a journal you may want to have a journal for your thoughts and a separate one for your prayers and gratitude list. Or, you may want to include your prayers and your gratitude list in your regular journal. You may want three separate journals; a prayer journal, a gratitude journal and a general one. I keep one journal that includes everything; I like simplicity. Whatever works the best for you is the way you should do it. The important thing is to write down your prayers, your gratitude list and your thoughts and feelings.

Some of the world's most respected and successful people have kept a journal. Albert Einstein, Marie Curie, Mark Twain, Thomas Edison, Frida Kahlo, Charles Darwin, and Leonardo da Vinci just to name a few. There is a saying, "Those who keep a journal live twice."

It would be good to end our prayers with a phrase such as, "this or something better for the good of all involved." Ending our prayers with this or a similar phrase will release the outcome of our prayers to the wisdom of God. We may be asking for a specific outcome for ourselves or another and at the same time our deepest heart's desire is for the manifestation of an outcome that is the absolute best for all involved. In short, we are free to ask for what we want and release the outcome without attachment. Or, we might pray, "Your perfect will be done." Because of embedded theology, you may think of God's will as being something that is automatically opposed to your own. You may think that "God's will" means that you have to do something hard that you do not want to do or something may be withheld from you that you truly desire. I invite you to let go of this difficult teaching. Why can't God's will and your will be the same?

We may know what we want at a given point in time but we may not know what would work out the best for ourselves and all others who are involved. "Your perfect will be done," or, "This or something better for the good of all involved," aligns our minds with the good that is already flowing to us through the wisdom of The Creator. By releasing the outcome we open ourselves to the possibility of a blessing much greater than we could think or imagine.

Meditation Practice

Meditation is when we listen to God in order to hear the "still, small voice" that speaks to us from within. We all need times of stillness and quiet. There are many forms of meditation that are being taught today and they all have merit. If you do not currently have a form of meditation that you adhere to, you might check out the library or internet about classes available in your area. There are also DVD's available that teach various forms of meditation. The important thing is to find one that suits you and practice it regularly. You may think that you are too busy for meditation. Being busy makes a regular meditation practice even more important. The busier you are the more you need a daily meditation practice. Twenty minutes, twice a day, is ideal for most people. If you think you can't manage that, then consider ten minutes twice a day. If you can't manage ten minutes, do five. The point is to meditate using the time that you make available and do it regularly. You will begin to look forward to your meditations and in time you will probably (eventually) add the time necessary to feel centered and at peace. A regular meditation practice has far reaching affects in keeping you calmly headed in the direction of your dreams.

Since 2005, my primary practice has been Insight Meditation. It is derived from an ancient form of meditation called Vipassana that was reintroduced by The Buddha. It is a practice of mindfulness and has no particular belief system attached to it, therefore, it can complement any set of spiritual beliefs. There are Insight Meditation centers and sanghas all over the world where this practice is taught. Many of these centers offer Insight Meditation Retreats as well. The Insight Meditation Retreat that is dear to my heart is the one that occurs twice a year at Unity Village, usually around April and October and is led by Reverend Robert Brumet.

Meditation is essential in *Living Full-Tilt.* We must take time regularly to center with Divine Energy. A daily, conscious contact with the God of our understanding is the foundation upon which our life grows. We must have that foundation in order to move in the direction of our dreams. It is my belief that regular meditation is not optional if we expect to live life to the fullest.

A daily meditation practice has many fringe benefits in addition to the obvious spiritual ones. Some of the benefits are:

- Stress reduction
- Regulated blood pressure
- Relief from insomnia
- Increased awareness of mind/body/spirit connection
- The ability to settle and identify feelings
- Anxiety relief
- Pain relief
- Relief from depression
- Strengthened immune system
- Increased cardiovascular health

We find over time that a regular meditation practice puts us in touch with wisdom from within that we may not know that we possess. It promotes an overall sense of calm that helps everything run more smoothly.

Even with a dedicated regular meditation practice, there comes a time when an extended period of meditation and solitude are very beneficial. In our busy world, taking time for solitude is a way to balance doing with being. The busier we are, the more we need to take time out. Taking time apart from our regular routine to step back and assess where we are in life is very beneficial. When we set a time to back away far enough to look at the bigger picture, we get a better perspective about all of life; not just our own. Looking at the larger picture goes a long way in helping us to stay focused on what is really important.

I will share with you a practice that helps me. I do this in addition to my regular Insight Meditation practice and Insight Meditation Retreats. I started this practice some years ago when I took a spiritual development class at Unity Village. The class was titled "Prayer". At the end of the class the instructor, Reverend Jim Rosemergy, issued a challenge to us. He said, "If you want to know God in a much deeper way there is a practice that will help you. Set aside at least three full days, longer if possible. Choose a place where you will be alone or at least a minimum of contact with people. This place should be quiet, devoid of distractions and with beautiful places to walk and sit. Choose either a place where your meals are provided or take simple food with you so that preparing meals does not take much of your time and does not distract you from your intended purpose. Take a minimum, but adequate, amount of comfortable clothing. Take a journal, a pen and nothing else. No books, CD's, TV, radio, phone, computer or electronics of any kind. In short, it's just you and God." He went on to say that the time would be best spent talking to God and listening to God and keeping a journal of all that comes up. In addition to prayers and thoughts that come in through meditation, write down all of your thoughts and feelings. Rev. Jim also said, "Call me when you are about to do it so that I can pray with you during that time."

This seemed huge to me. I had taken personal silent, retreats in the past and loved them. There is something in me that is naturally drawn to the silence. But, in years past while on silent retreats I always had spiritually based books, tapes, CD's, etc. Whereas, the time away from my usual surroundings and regular routine was great and felt very spiritually nourishing, I had never been without stimuli of some kind on these personal silent retreats.

It took me a while to find the time and to get up the courage to do this three day silent retreat where only God and I were invited. I called Rev. Jim as he had requested and set out on this adventure.

I chose a place where I had gone many times before but under different circumstances. It is named The Christian Renewal Center. It is not far outside of the town where I lived but had the feeling of being very remote. When I turned off the street, next to the sign that bore its name, the road narrowed and became a gravel road. Further down the road it became a dirt road complete with well-traveled ruts. For the entire length of the road there was a canopy of beautiful trees. As I drove further, the trees and bushes created a dense forest effect. After about a mile, I came to an opening and off to the left were buildings and a parking lot. It is my understanding that this center was originally built as a retreat place for Catholic priests and later was opened up to other activities as well. The buildings appeared as though they may have been built in the 1960's and looked very inviting and tranquil. There was a main building, two chapels, various meeting rooms and a motel-like building. It was quiet and felt very peaceful. It was like a breath of fresh air. My key was waiting for me on a bulletin board outside the office. I took the key and went to my room and got settled in.

The staff was alerted when there was a person on a personal, silent retreat. Care was taken to do a minimum of talking. Not long after I arrived, dinner was served. I looked forward to the meals because, through past experience, I knew the food was delicious.

After the first few hours, I felt awkward and a little fear came up about what I might discover in this time of silence. I spent time in prayer. I sat in meditation. I wrote about it. And then I thought, "Now what?" I had made a commitment to stay three days. I do not take my commitments lightly, so I knew that I would stay but what next? I walked the beautiful grounds, I prayed, I meditated and I wrote. I had thoughts about my businesses, my family, my relationships, my pets, my house, my life in general and wondered if I could have spent this time in a more beneficial way with books and recordings. The time passed and I began to feel more relaxed. I became more at peace than I had been in a very long time. I wrote thoughts in those pages; many of which did not seem like my own thoughts. I felt amazed that some of those words were penned by me. I ate, I slept, I walked, I did yoga, I prayed, I meditated and I wrote. I started to feel at home in my own skin (a feeling that I lost some time ago). On the third day, I woke up and started to think with dread that I would be leaving. I tried to think of a way that I could stay longer but I had only made arrangements for three days. My businesses and my pets needed my attention. There were things that I needed do. So, I stayed as late in the day as I dared and then went home. As I drove home, there was a bittersweet feeling. Bitter because I wanted to stay longer and sweet because I had found a new practice that filled my heart to overflowing and had given me a profound sense of peace in my otherwise turbulent life. I felt a deeper connection with God. I know that God is always with me and always within me, but I felt much more aware of that Divine Presence. I began planning my next trip back and I told myself that next time I would take longer than three days. I was hooked! I could not wait to tell Rev. Jim about my experience. I left with an understanding of why he said at least three days. It took the full three days for me to get to the quiet place within me where there is only peace. I have heard this place of peace described as that place within that "water cannot wet, wind cannot dry, fire cannot burn and weapons cannot destroy". I had, indeed, been to that place. I will be forever grateful to Reverend Jim Rosemergy for issuing the challenge to our class. Because of my silent retreats, my life is rich in ways that I could never have imagined.

I have since moved out of the area of the Christian Renewal Center but I bring my memories with me. When I arrived at my new home, one of the first things I did was to look for a place to take my silent retreats. Through a series of seeming chance encounters, I found my new favorite place to take my silent retreats. At this point in my life, my silent retreats are not optional. They are essential to my physical, mental, emotional and spiritual well-being. Now that I have experienced the richness of the silence and the incredible closeness with my Creator, I am pulled from within to these times of silent communion.

My new favorite place is a monastery. I have no Catholic background and yet I love this place! It is about an hour's drive from my home and very secluded. To get there, I drive down a main highway, turn into the narrow streets of a small town and then onto a road named "Toe Nail Trail." I have asked, but no one seems to know where this road got its name. Maybe someday I will find out. I travel about thirty minutes on Toe Nail Trail until I see a very small sign that reads, "Our Lady of Grace Carmelite Monastery." Then I turn down a dirt and gravel road and travel another fifteen or twenty minutes before finally reaching the monastery. On this dirt and gravel road, there are very few buildings visible. Mostly what I see are mesquite trees, cactus, cattle, sheep, goats and an occasional llama. The monastery was founded in 1989 and the buildings resemble old Spanish style. It is the home of a group of the most wonderful and precious Carmelite nuns. They are a cloistered order and live in a fenced-off part of the monastery. In the front of the main building there is one small room with a bathroom that is lodging for personal retreats. It has everything that I need; a comfortable single bed, a desk, a chair, a wardrobe, a microwave, a small refrigerator and a coffee pot. Most of the time when I stay, I am the only one there other than the nuns. It is paradise to me and perfect for my silent retreats. There is no TV or radio in the room, no Wi-Fi and no cell phone coverage. That releases me from any temptation to do anything other than commune with God. I go to mass in the mornings in the beautiful, rustic-style chapel. It feels very sacred and holy. I am not Catholic so I cannot receive communion but I get in line with the others and when it is my turn, the priest places his hand on my head and gives me a blessing. Sometimes I am the only one in attendance for mass other than the nuns and the priest. I usually stay after mass is over and write about my experience in my journal. I do not want to lose any of the details because God usually speaks to me during mass, but I wait until mass is over to do my writing. I find that if I want to write about an experience, the magic of the perfect words begins to dissipate if I wait too long, so I write as soon as possible. I love to capture the depth of my experiences and allow the words to pour forth. I know that it is The Divine expressing through me and I love to let it flow. The feeling of having the words flow through me is exquisite. It is like intense love manifesting in every cell of my body.

The monastery is so remote and secluded that silence is the order of the day and night. I love to walk the trails in all directions. Sometimes I find a large rock and sit down and meditate or write in my journal. Several of us, who frequent the monastery, pooled our money and bought a bench for the yard. We placed it under the trees. It is light-weight and I can easily move it around. There is a statue of the Virgin Mary, under a pergola, just past a small grove of trees. I often sit in front of it to do my writing. I sometimes wonder what her life was **really** like.

I have stayed there many times in the years that I have lived in the area. I have stayed as many as five days in a row and I have yet to feel like it is ever long enough. The silence is wonderful. The nuns are wonderful. The buildings are comforting. My experience with mass and the singing, praying and chanting of the nuns is heavenly. I have found my new favorite place for my silent retreats.

Daily meditation is very important to me. The days that I spend in silence and solitude with only a pen and a journal are very precious to me. Both meditation and solitude are necessary to my spiritual, mental, emotional and physical well-being. I have come to the place in my life where I know, beyond a shadow of a doubt, that meditation, silence and solitude are not optional for me. I require those times when all of the extraneous details of life are stripped away and it is just God and me. It is in those times that I *know* oneness and that it is not God and me; it is God/me.

My Gratitude

I am so very grateful to be doing the work that I am doing! This is work that I would do without pay if my finances would allow it. I am so grateful for my life. My core life's purpose is to encourage others. I have known this for many years. In ministry I have a multitude of opportunities to encourage and uplift others as they go through the struggles of life. I also have the opportunity to encourage and uplift people who want to move forward in their lives and may be feeling the fear of getting outside their comfort zone. I have had so many of the life experiences that people struggle with and seem to want help. There are very few situations in which I counsel others that I have not experienced myself. Having had similar experiences gives me an insight into some of what they may be feeling. I get to celebrate with them when they become more than they ever thought they could be even in their wildest imagination!

When I conduct my *Living Full-Tilt Workshops,* I get to help people see and know who they really are, Precious Expressions of The Most High God, Points of Light within The Greater Light. When people come to me after the workshop and talk to me about a break-through that they had or an "a-ha" moment, it is confirmation to me that I am in my right and perfect place, doing what is mine to do in this world. It is like getting a B-12 shot! It energizes me and gives me a sense of well-being to know that I am squarely in the middle of "who I came here to be"!

Even in the midst of living the life of our dreams, there will probably be challenges and situations that are not to our liking. Such is life. Even though I know that I am in my right place, doing what I am called to do, every single thing about my life is not a bed of roses. But there is always the underlying knowing that I have answered and continue to answer the call of my life. For that, I bless *all* of my life experiences. This is quite a departure from my lowest points when I wanted to end my life. It took some time and work for me to get from there to here but the time and effort was more than worth it. I am so very grateful for my life. I am so grateful that my life experiences help me to be more compassionate and understanding of those who come to me with similar experiences.

Affirmations

Only good comes to me in my life.

I am blessed beyond measure.

I have more than enough for myself and to share.

Chapter IV

Giving and Receiving

Two Sides of the Same Coin

"A generous heart, kind speech, and a life of service and compassion are the things that renew humanity."

Buddha

An acorn must be given to fertile ground to grow a mighty oak tree. As in nature, we must first give in order to receive.

Janie Kelley

God is My Source

Whatever name we give to The Power greater than anything, it is of paramount importance that we recognize and acknowledge It as our Source. There are many channels through which our prosperity may come but it comes from the One True Source. We may look at our paycheck, the company, the boss, the economy, AMEX, a family member, our business, Social

Security, a trust fund or something similar as our source. However, these are simply channels through which our good comes. They are not the source. By acknowledging God as our One True Source we place ourselves in the flow of good. The wonderful news is that, "It is God's good pleasure to give us the kingdom." God is our source and is constantly pouring out blessings to us. It is up to each of us to do what is ours to do in order to be open and receptive to our good! We must follow spiritual laws governing wealth as we understand them today.

Think of the flow of money like the flow of a body of water. Just as a body of water must have an inlet and an outlet to flow, so must we keep money in circulation in order to receive more and remain in the flow. If we want water to flow, we must give it room and it must not be dammed-up. What happens to water when it is dammed up? It becomes stagnant and cannot support the usual life forms. The same is true about money and material wealth. If we stop the flow of money by failing to give, as well as receive, it becomes stagnant and cannot support its usual life forms. If we want a continuous flow of material abundance, money must not be stopped at any point. It must flow in and out of our lives unimpeded. A portion of all that we receive must be given away. It must be given away with no strings attached. If there are strings attached to our giving, it is not a gift but a bribe or a payoff.

The same concept is true of any good thing in your life. Whatever you want, give it. If you want more love in your life, give it. If you want more peace in your life, give it. If you want more understanding in your life, give it. It is true in the material world, as well. If you want more money in your life, you must first give it.

The universal law of giving and receiving is like the law of gravity. You don't have to believe in it for it to work. You don't even have to know about it for it to work. And, it works the same for everyone.

If you lean forward far enough in the chair in which you sit, you will fall. Gravity does not care who you are, what you have accomplished, what mistakes you have made, how very witty you are, how boring you are, what talent you have or how good looking you are, you will fall if you lean forward far enough in your chair. It is the same with the law of giving and receiving. The law of giving and receiving works whether you believe in it or not, whether you know about it or not and it works for everyone.

What you give out is what you get back. Every major world religion teaches this because it is a capital "T" Truth. A capital "T" Truth is Truth which does not change. There is relative truth, or personal truth, that is changeable. "Broccoli doesn't taste good." That is my personal truth. It is not a capital "T" Truth because many people like the taste of broccoli. "God is the source of all good"; is a capital "T" Truth because it is universal and unchanging.

The Law of Giving and Receiving is a capitol "T" Truth. It is very simple. What we give out is what we get back. If we give out good, we get back good. If we give out generously, we receive generously. If we give help to others, we receive help from others. We may not receive from the same source that we have given but we receive back in like kind nevertheless. And, the opposite is also true. If we give with scarcity, we get back with scarcity. If we give out in a consciousness of lack and contraction, what we get back is lack and contraction. If we give out negativity, what we get back is more negativity. In my belief system, the only exception would be that goodness and generosity come with a much higher vibration. A higher vibration always trumps a lower vibration.

The good in our world is much more powerful than that which falls short of good. Good is like light. Negativity is like darkness. The speed of light can be measured because it is a form of energy and is a living thing. The speed of darkness cannot be measured because it has no power or energy of its own; therefore, it is "no-thing." It is simply the absence of light. Negativity, scarcity, limitation, and such have no real power of their own. So goodness, generosity, limitlessness, and similar traits have a much higher level of vibration. Meaning, we do not always get back negativity equal to that which we send out. Some might call this "The Grace of God." By the Grace of God, we are spared some of the repercussions of our negative acts and negative thoughts.

Living Full-Tilt includes many other things, but our focus here will be placed on money. Money plays such a significant role in our lives that our money needs to be on solid ground so that we are not giving an inordinate amount of our time, focus and creative energy to it. Every area of our lives is affected in some way by money. When we master money and materiality, our creative energy is freed up so that we can be our true creative self. When we have mastered money, we are in a much better position to take advantage of life's opportunities; we are freer to help others and we are more open to give the gift of who we are to the world. We are meant to shine and live lives of opulence and plenty!

Just as there are two sides to a coin, giving and receiving are two sides of the "coin" of opulent living. If I had the proper tools, I could slice a coin but it would still have two sides. I could take another slice and it would still have two sides. I could not slice a coin thin enough to eliminate one of its sides. The same is true with giving and receiving. They are inseparable. You cannot have one without the other.

Giving must take place first to set into motion the Spiritual Law of Giving and Receiving. An acorn must be given to fertile ground to grow a mighty oak tree. Likewise, as in nature, we must first give in order to receive. You may be saying to yourself, "I have nothing to give." Be assured that you always have something to give. Even if you have absolutely no money at all, you have something of material value to start the flow of material wealth to you. You have an article of clothing or a household item to donate, a casserole to share with a friend, a piece of jewelry to give away, a ride to the market for someone who needs it, flowers from your yard or wild flowers, a Thank You note, etc. Use your imagination and you will come up with something. When you give something of monetary value, open your mind and heart to see what comes back to you in return because the universe will not slight you. When you receive your return, give again. You have just set into motion the Universal Law of Giving and Receiving! You must continue to give in order to continue to receive. If you were to stop giving, it would interrupt the flow and the flow would eventually stop. You will not stop giving because you have proven to yourself that the Law of Giving and Receiving really does work! Keep a small notebook of your giving and receiving. You will see how you're giving, as well as your receiving, will gain in value. As time goes by, you will find that you have more and more to give, which begins to include money.

Receiving Generously

We must learn to give, and give generously, in order to stay in the flow of our good. We must also learn to receive generously. Many prosperity teachers teach the importance of giving in order to receive. Giving is not optional in living a life of opulence because it keeps us in the flow of prosperity. We must also receive generously in order to stay in the flow. We must open wide our lives and prepare to receive the abundance of the universe. It is possible to give and give and give and still not receive if we are not open and receptive when the good comes to us. By not receiving our good we dam up the flow. *We must become bold and generous receivers.* Remember, there is no lack in the universe. There may be a false perception that looks like lack, but that is only the relative world view. It is not the Truth. We may not allow ourselves to receive because we see lack in the world. When we believe in lack, we block the receiving of our own good. The Truth is that the supply of God's substance is limitless; it has no end.

"The inexhaustible resource of Spirit is equal to every demand. There is no reality in lack. Abundance is here and now manifest!" Charles Fillmore

We must always remember that our Creator is the One True Source. There is no other. We have many possible channels through which our good may come to us, but God is The One True Source.

If you are currently struggling with money or have ever struggled with money, you know that the experience is exhausting and debilitating. It is exhausting to worry about how to pay the mortgage, electric bill, gas bill, phone bill, credit card bills, medical bills, car repair bills, and still put food on the table. It depletes our creative energy. Worrying about money when there never seems to be enough is demeaning and depressing. It perpetuates thoughts of unworthiness. When we are feeling these negative emotions, there is little or no room for joy in our lives. Our physical energy is also reduced because of this mental and emotional drain. If the struggle with money goes on for an extended period of time, it begins to affect every area of our lives.

When stable finances are in place, our energy is freed up so that we can live the life of our dreams. When we master money and materiality, our energy is then released to move openly in the other areas of our lives. Our creative energy can go to our relationships, hobbies that make our heart sing, activities which deepen our connection with Spirit, enjoying a nice vacation, soaking up nature and being all that we came to this planet to be!

The Truth is: There is no reality in lack! Think about a time in your life when money was not a serious issue. Maybe there was a time when money was not an issue at all. How was your life then? How was your physical energy level? What do you remember about your emotions? Were you in touch with your innate joy? Did you feel freer? Answer these questions with rigorous honesty and you will have some insight into how money, or the lack thereof, affects your life.

Just as there was a time when money was of little or no issue, it will be again in an even better way. This time you will have mastered the energy of money and you will keep your eyes on The One True Source. This time you will follow the spiritual principles governing money that are outlined in this book and your mind and heart will be open to the guidance of Spirit in your life. Once these spiritual principles are a part of your life, opulence will become a way of life. You will have all that you desire and more! You will be in a place to share your abundance with the world and never run out because, "The inexhaustible Resource of Spirit is equal to every demand!" You will recognize and know yourself for who you really are; a son or daughter of the Most High. You will really get it that the unlimited substance of the universe has no end. Aligning yourself with spiritual principles places you squarely in the flow of unlimited universal substance!

We must open ourselves to Divine guidance when giving. When we are open, we will be guided to give generously from our abundance. It may take time and we may learn it by degrees, but, if we commit to giving, the ultimate outcome will be open generosity. When we listen to our guidance we often find that we are guided to be more and more generous. Eventually, we find that we are giving more than we could ever have imagined. We find that the more we give the more we get. The more we get the more we have to give. We are no longer giving from fear and scarcity, we are giving from opulence!

The world's wealthiest people know the importance of giving as well as receiving. There are millionaires and billionaires who give away up to 90% of their wealth on a regular basis and still have far more than they will ever spend. They started out giving smaller gifts, just like you. If you think you will wait to give generously until you reach a certain level of wealth, you are likely fooling yourself. Having more money will not magically make you a generous person. If you start now being generous with what you currently have, the universe will supply you with more with which to be generous.

In order to live a life of opulence, we must learn to be generous givers and generous receivers. We must open ourselves wide to the possibilities of life. We must let go of feeling undeserving and know that prosperity in all things is our birthright.

How do you receive a compliment? Do you deflect it or attempt to neutralize it? Or, do you look the person in the eye, take a breath and allow yourself to absorb what has been said? Receiving a compliment is good practice for receiving money. We must first be master over the small things so that we can be master over larger things. One way in which we prepare our consciousness is by stretching ourselves in small ways. The next time someone gives you a compliment, notice your reaction. Even if you don't deflect it with your words, do you really let it in? Notice any contraction of muscles in your stomach, neck, arms or any other part of your body. Contracting of muscles is a physical manifestation of contracting thoughts. When you are given a compliment do you "check out" mentally so that you do not allow your mind to take it in? Or, do you remain fully present to the moment and absorb the full intention of the compliment? When money comes to you in large amounts will your consciousness be open enough to receive it?

Give and It Shall Be Given

"Give and it will be given unto you. A good measure; pressed down, shaken together and running over it will be put into your lap, for the measure that you give is the measure you will get back." Luke 6:38 (NRSV)

Notice the first word, "give." Notice that we are instructed first to give and then it will be given to us. We are to make the first move. The Universe is waiting for us to start the flow of money and all good things. Many of life's blessings come in this manner. We pray for a new job, and the Universe says "Yes, and send out resumes." Much of the time, the first step in receiving is ours. The Universe is waiting to give us our heart's desires, "good measure pressed down, shaken together and running over," as soon as we make a move in a forward direction. I find that most of the blessings that have come into my life have required that I make a move of some kind. Something is required of me. It is as though the Universe is asking, "Do you really mean it?"

I was raised in the country, for which I am exceedingly grateful. There are many wonderful things about living close to nature. There are many of life's metaphysical lessons which can be learned in nature if one is awake to it.

When I was a child, we had a hand pump just outside the back door. It was the kind with the handle that must be pumped up and down to get water. Unless you have been around such a pump, you may think that you just walk up and pump the handle and water flows out. That would not be the whole story. If the pump has not been used in a day or even a few hours the pump must be primed. In order to prime the pump, water must be poured into the opening of the pump to fill up the space and create a vacuum. You must put water in before you can get water out. It is the same way with money. The Universe is waiting for you to "prime the pump." Furthermore, once the flow starts, we must continue by giving on a regular basis. As with the hand pump, if you stop the flow you will eventually lose the "prime."

When we know how spiritual principles work, we have the opportunity to work with them to achieve whatever is our heart's desire. Just like the laws of physics, we must work with the law to get the desired result. We could say to the hand pump, "First give me some water and then I will put water in. I am afraid if I give you my water you will not give any back to me. If I use up all of my water and you don't give any back, then what will I do? Just go ahead and give me some water and I promise I will give some back to you." We could argue with the pump and plead with it forever and it would not make any difference because that is not how the pump works. We may have a similar situation with money. "What if I give money and I don't get anything back? What if my giving takes me down to my last dime? What will I do?" We can say to the universe, "I promise that I will give generously if only you will first send me lots of money." There are physical laws that govern how the hand pump will work and there are spiritual laws that govern how money works. We must first give and then we will receive.

Once the flow is going you must continually be in the flow of money in order to continue to receive on a regular basis. Remember, wealth is your birthright.

Tithing

The word tithe means 10%. A definition of tithing is to give 10% of all of the money you receive to the person, group of people, church or organization where you have received spiritual inspiration. Spiritual inspiration is that which serves to raise your consciousness and reminds you of who you really are.

Tithing is a practice dating back thousands of years. In essence, it is giving 10% to support spiritual work in the world. When you have received spiritual inspiration, it is only natural to want to support the person or organization to be able to continue such work that will in turn serve others as you have been served. If the teachings you received were valuable to you, these teachings will probably be valuable to others, as well. Tithing is a way of seeing that these teachings continue. Giving to charities and various organizations is a good practice but it is not tithing in the strictest sense. Tithing is a way of saying, "Thank You," and supporting the work of the person or organization where you have received spiritual nourishment. It is a proven way to place yourself squarely in the flow of the goodness that is yours by Divine Right. Malachi 3:10 states it this way, "Bring all of the tithes into the storehouse that there may be food in my house and test me now in this, says the Lord of Hosts, if I will not open the windows of heaven and pour out a blessing for you that there will not room enough to receive it." (MEV)

- The Magic Number of Increase

I have been asked, "Why 10%?" I have asked other spiritual teachers the same question. Why not 5%, or 8% or 12 1/2 %? I will give you the same answer that was given to me by my prosperity teachers; "I don't know!"! The giving of 10% of all that one has received has been practiced for thousands of years with great success and is taught by many of the world's religions. Ten percent has been called "the magic number of increase" by some of our richest ancient civilizations. In ancient times, the teaching was to give ten percent of the best of crops, cattle, olive oil, silver, gold, or whatever was used as currency. This was seen as thanking God for continued increase in their lives. Many people have become incredibly wealthy by using this ancient law of increase. Many wealthy people today attribute their wealth to this ancient, proven law. Today, what I know for sure is that tithing works for me.

Tithing 10% is a good place to start. Once you see that tithing really works to bring wealth into your life, you will find yourself giving even more.

Giving is not optional! If we are to get into the flow and stay in the flow of wealth we must give and give regularly. If we give sporadically, we will receive sporadically.

Money is a Tool

Money is a tool not a goal. It is a means to an end, not the end itself. The whole point is not just to see how much money we can amass. Money is just green paper. The value of money comes in what money can buy and the opportunities it affords. Money itself is neutral. In and of itself, it means nothing. It is the person or people in charge of the money who gives it worth.

When we practice the spiritual principles that place us in the flow of money, we will be in charge of various amounts. It is through guidance that we know how to distribute the money that we have. The Still Small Voice will guide us to do what is ours to do with the money that has been entrusted to us.

Genuine inner guidance from God will direct the flow. We need only surrender it to the God of our understanding and be open to hear the answer. We will know what the answer is from The Divine because it will be beneficial and will ultimately bring joy, peace or both.

Tithing at Luby's

I was very impressed with a story of tithing told to me by my spiritual teacher and mentor, Edwene Gaines. She practices tithing to the person, place or institution where she receives her spiritual food. Her story was about having tithed to a waitress in a coffee shop because this waitress had blessed her with encouraging words at a low time in her life.

When I owned my businesses, I often ate lunch at a nearby Luby's Cafeteria because the food was fresh and I could eat and get back to work in a reasonable period of time. There I met a woman who pushed the tea cart. Her job was to go around the dining room and make sure that the customers had plenty of tea, coffee, napkins and such. Each day we would talk a little and I got to know her and a few things about her life. She was born in Japan and she had come to the United States so that she could work and send money back to her family. Her ultimate goal was to have enough money to bring her family to the United States. After numerous conversations, I suppose she began to feel a measure of trust in me and one day she decided to tell me more of her story. She talked about her faith in God and that she knew that one day she and her family would be reunited. At that time, she lived in a rented room so she could send most of the money to her family and she saved what she could for the day when they would all be together. I was so moved and inspired by her story and her faith in God to bring her family together that I decided to give a part of my tithe to her. The next time I went in, I placed a $100 bill in a greeting card and took it with me. (Back then, $100 was worth a lot more than it is today.) Just before leaving I walked over to her and placed it in her hand. I quickly walked away because I did not want it to be a scene. I have no idea what her reaction was because I was gone before she could get the envelope open. I felt such a sense of having done what was mine to do in that situation. Sometimes God moves our hearts to do a certain thing that is out of the ordinary but in complete alignment with our sense of personal integrity. That was one of the high points of my early tithing history.

I am sometimes asked, "When I give, is it okay to expect to receive?" My answer is emphatically, "Yes!" As you give, so do you receive. You reap what you sow. The measure you give is the measure you receive. You get back what you give out. Many scriptures and sacred writings tell us that we receive as a result of giving. Every major world religion teaches this. There is every reason to expect our good to come to us when we are in accordance with spiritual principles. Be open; your good may come in unexpected ways!

If you are experiencing lack in finances in any form, begin to give immediately. If you already are in the habit of giving, then give thought and be in prayer about giving more generously. Remember we get back what we give out.

Affirmations

I give freely, joyously and generously. I receive freely, joyously and generously.

I open myself to receive all of the good that is here for me.

I openly accept my life of freedom, joy and plenty.

CHAPTER V

What Do You Want?

"Shoot for the moon. Even if you miss you will land among the stars."

Les Brown

"You are not meant to live a mediocre life. Like the stars, you are meant to SHINE!"

Janie Kelley

Heart's Desires

What do you want? What do you *really* want? Not what someone else wants for you; not what you are expected to want but what is it that you *really, really* want? These are your heart's desires. Your heart's desires are placed within you by God. Along with these heart's desires comes everything that you will ever need to bring them into manifestation. Everything you may think you want is not necessarily your heart's desire. Ordinary wants come and go. A true heart's desire is an unmistakable urge that comes from deep within. A true heart's desire is often connected to your life's purpose and is meant to be fulfilled. God will not place within you a heart's desire and then say to you, "Too bad you don't have what it takes to manifest this desire. I'd like to help you but you're on your own with this one." Of course not! God gives, generously, so that we can fulfill our heart's desires. We need only open ourselves to receive.

Do not hesitate to ask for what you want! Jesus said, *"Ask,* and it shall be given unto you. *Seek,* and you shall find. *Knock,* and the door shall be opened to you. For everyone who asks, receives. All those who seek, find. To those who knock, the door shall be opened." Matthew 7:7-12

It is perfectly natural to desire a better life. It is perfectly natural to desire forward movement in life. If it were not for the desire within human beings for a better life we would still be living in caves and chasing down our food. Without that natural desire for improvement there would be no new inventions. We would not have cars, phones, electricity, computers, homes, and many things which make our lives richer and enable us to do tasks in a much more efficient way. If it were not for the innate desire for better, we would probably be without language. Charles Fillmore wrote, "Desire is the onward impulse of the ever-evolving soul". This desire moves us into greater and greater levels of consciousness as well. The inner urge to be better propels us to study, pray, meditate, go to classes, teach classes and in many ways move toward a closer conscious relationship with The Divine. Since the beginning of recorded history, humankind has sought to have a more intimate relationship with the God of their understanding. That "onward impulse" has taken us from worshipping stones, lightening, fire and the like to a moment by moment conscious awareness of the Divine that is within each and every one of us. We have only begun to understand the nature and scope of our Creator. "Eye hath not seen nor ear heard, neither have entered into the heart of man the things which God hath prepared for those that love Him." I Corinthians 2:9 (KJV)

It is God's good pleasure to give us the kingdom, so, why not ask for what you want! What would you ask for if you were brave? What would you ask for if you knew the answer was "yes?" Go for it!

"So let us come boldly to the very throne of God and stay there to receive his mercy and find grace to help us in our times of need." Hebrews 4:16 (TLB)

What do you want? Many people know more about what they don't want than what they do want. *We tell the universe what we want by giving our attention to it.* We "vote" with our thoughts and words. When we give our attention to that which we don't want we are still giving it our vote. We are telling the Universe we want more. Worry is a form of focused attention. We would do well to take our attention away from that which we don't want and place it on that which we do want. Where our thoughts go our life flows.

Working with Universal Law

When we work with the principles of the universe, we allow ourselves to be in harmony with the flow. It is not necessary for us to like a principle, to believe in it or even know about it for it to work. If we are to have the positive changes that we want to see in our lives, we must work with the universal principles that have the power to affect the change we seek.

It is up to you to learn the principles that govern our wonderful universe so that you can cooperate with them. It is your choice. You can do what you have always done and you will get what you have always gotten. Or, you can commit to a period of time of putting these spiritual principles into action and see the results.

Raise Your Level of Expectancy

Do you have a vision of your heart's desire? Does it seem doable without much difficulty? If so, it is probably too small! Sometimes we set our visions too low because we have been told that anything larger would be foolish or just plain impossible. We sometimes succumb to the opinions of others and allow mediocrity to set in. Or, we set our sights too low because we have been taught that it will save us from disappointment. We are told, "Don't get your hopes up". We are trained to protect ourselves from hurt and we buy into the idea that we are better off. When we play it safe and protect ourselves from hurt and disappointment, we also protect ourselves from reaching the high level of living that we are meant to experience. The result can be a life of dull, mid-range mediocrity. I say, **"Get your hopes up! Get your hopes up every day!"**

I don't think that you got up one morning and said to yourself, "I think that I will live a life of dull, mid-range mediocrity and always do and be less than I am capable of. Not only will I not be and do all that I am capable of, I will accept this way of life and call it normal." Of course you didn't! You started out your life as a child with really big dreams. You knew in your heart-of-hearts that you could do anything that you set your mind to. That part of you that had this knowing is still within you! You are meant to live a life of joy and opulence and on some level you still know that! You are meant to shine in this world in whatever way you choose. You know it or you would not have made it this far into this book! On some level you have always known this is true. You may have lost sight of it but deep within your heart it is still there.

We buy into the pattern of what the world believes is rational and normal. In his book, *The Four Agreements*, Don Miguel Ruiz calls this "the domestication of humans." Just as animals are domesticated and tamed by training we become domesticated and tamed by agreeing with the collective consciousness about what is acceptable and what is not. Even though the concepts we were taught may be deeply ingrained, we still have a choice about whether or not to continue to let them rule our lives. We can break away from the mediocre and reconnect with our original self. We can co-create with God for the life that we really love living. Remember, "If you want to taste the fruit of the tree you have to go out on a limb."

Raise your level of expectancy! Allow yourself to expect the best! God wants more for you than you could possibly imagine. Give God a chance to fulfill your heart's desires. Don't limit God!

God placed, within you, beautiful desires of your heart and then gave you everything you need to bring these desires to fruition. It is up to you to use all that you have been given. You need only step up and receive what is yours by Divine Right. Chances are great that the first step is up to you. Maybe Spirit has done what It is going to do until you make the next move. God is just waiting for you to take the next step. Set your intentions high and step out in faith!

When I was accepted into seminary, I set about to tell people in my life about my decision. Prior to that time, I had only confided in people who needed to know what I was doing, specifically, my minister and a few others in my church. After my acceptance, I set about to inform my family, clients and friends. Over the years, a few of my clients had become my friends. That was the case with two of my clients who were each other's best friend. They each had become my friend, as well. The two of them got together and bought a gift for me as a going-away present. It turns out that the gift probably meant more to me over the next few years than they ever could have imagined. The gift was a plaque that was done by an artist. It has an unusual look to it. The plaque reads, "Leap and The Net Will Appear." There is a drawing of a person leaping in the air. I put that plaque on the wall opposite my bed during the entire time I was in seminary. Many times I would look at it for inspiration and feel the love that went into the gift given to me by my friends. Since then, I have been inspired many times, by Divine guidance, to leap and the "net" always appears. That plaque now hangs in my office.

Look into your heart and see what is there. Chances are great that there is a dream in there that is so big that, only by the Grace of God will you ever achieve it. That is the one to go for! Stretch your faith and allow Spirit to help you. Step out and follow the dream that God gave you. **You are worth it!**

You may have heard it said, "Step to the edge of the light that you see." This is a popular way of saying, step out in faith. I say, when you hear the unmistakable guidance of Spirit, "Step **past** the edge of the light that you see." That is deep faith. Sometimes it takes deep faith to follow the deepest desire of your heart and to step past the edge of the light that you see with the assurance that God will be there. "When you get to the end of all the light that you know and it is time to step into the darkness of the unknown, faith is knowing that one of two things will happen; either you will be given something solid to stand on or you will be taught how to fly." Edward Teller

When you look in your heart and see the big dream that God has placed there, knowing that your Loving Creator has given you everything you will ever need to bring this dream to fruition, there is no reason to hesitate! If not now, when?

You are not meant to live a life of mediocrity! God did not create you to come here to planet Earth and live your whole life in struggle and hardship. You are meant for much more than a life of barely getting by, marking time in a job that does not inspire you, just making it from one day to the next. NO!!! You are here to have whatever makes your heart sing! Be Bold! Ask for what you want! Go "boldly before the throne of God"!

Jesus said, *"…let your light shine before others that they may see your good works and give glory to your Father who is in heaven"* Matthew 5:16 (ESV) What better way to glorify God than to live the life of your dreams! Imagine the happiness that you will spread (because it is contagious, you know) when you are happy with your own life! By living the life of your dreams you silently give others permission to go for their big dream as well! Just think about a world that is populated by happy people who are freely going for their big dream!

We each have different heart's desires according to who we are. Our heart's desires are like our fingerprints. Some may be similar but no two are exactly alike. There may be steps that you are required to take and work that you need to do, but when you are in alignment with God's desires for you, there will not be struggle. There may be some effort involved but not struggle. Much of the time there are tasks to be done and commitments to be made on your part, but if there is struggle involved, it is probably time to step back and take a good look at the situation. There may be undue worry and attempts to control the outcome. It could also mean that the heart's desire itself, while genuine and valid, needs to be approached in a different way. Ask for guidance and remain open. When the heart's desire and the method of achieving it are in sync with the Universal Mind there will be a flow of energy that you can recognize as God-Energy. It will bring peace and joy to your heart and mind.

Be Specific

Do not hesitate to ask for exactly what you want! There may be fear about asking for something that might not be for your highest good. Remember to say, "This or something better for the good of all involved." That statement releases the outcome to the wisdom of God. You may be asking yourself, "What if I get what I am asking for and I don't like it? What if I change my mind?" If that happens you say prayers of release, let it go and then make a different decision.

There are times in life that we let fear of making the wrong decision stand in our way of making any decision at all. Not making a conscious, pro-active decision is making a decision to allow past conditioning to take over.

If we are hazy and unclear about what we want, how is the universe going to deliver it? If we send out unclear or mixed messages we will get unclear or mixed results. The universe responds in like kind.

The getting of stuff is not our highest aim in life. But, why not experience fun and excitement while we are moving along our spiritual path here on earth. Yes, there are areas of life we would do well to take seriously but the seriousness of life needs to be balanced out with fun. Having some of life's comforts and toys can be relaxing and rejuvenating. "A cheerful heart is good medicine..." Proverbs 17:22 (ASV)

Allow yourself to dream big. Get in touch with the part of you that knows you not only deserve good gifts but also the part of you that knows that you can have what you want. Allow yourself to receive all that God has for you in this life. Open yourself to the "Big Dream!" Allow yourself to visualize your life as you really want it to be. Pull out all of the stops! Allow your imagination to soar! Don't limit God!

Your old paradigm will try to cut you off at every turn. Your old way of thinking has made a place for itself as the false ego and it does not want to give that up. Remember that **your best thinking of the past has gotten you where you are today**. Cast your net wider! You must incorporate broader more expansive thinking in order to make the changes that you want to see in your life. Begin to think differently. Begin to speak differently. Begin to act differently.

When you begin to think differently, speak differently and act differently the old paradigm will pop up and tell you all of the reasons that you are not good enough, talented enough, sharp enough and that you are too old, too young, too short, too tall, the wrong gender, the wrong race and all of the other reasons it will not work. Do not resist it or struggle with it. To struggle or resist gives it more of your energy. *What we resist persists.* Tell your false ego, "Thank you for sharing but I have a more expansive plan," and allow it to pass from your mind. Then go back to the capital "T" Truth of who you are. You are a precious child of God and you deserve all good. Do not give your false ego any energy and it will go back into the nothingness from whence it came. Act yourself into a new way of being! Soon you will not be acting; you will be living the life you love!

Chicken House Thinking

I grew up in the country in a house near my maternal grandparents. They always had a large garden, fruit trees and grapes growing on an arbor. My grandma had a milk cow and she raised chickens. As a child I was considered a tomboy. I climbed trees, made forts out of tree branches and blankets, shot marbles, played backyard sports and I would run, not walk, most everywhere I went. We did not have much in the way of playground equipment so we improvised. My grandparents had a chicken house at the end of their back yard and I spent a lot of time on top of it. Climbing was one of my favorite sports.

When I was three, four and five years old, I was convinced that I could do absolutely anything! I just knew it! Deep within me I just knew that there was nothing that I could not do. If my parents would just stop telling me that I couldn't and leave me alone for a while I would prove to them I was right! If they would just get out of my way I would show them that I could do anything! Being a tenacious child (that sounds so much more sophisticated than saying I was stubborn) I silently believed that if I climbed on top of the chicken house, jumped off and waved my arms in the air I could fly. After all, I had seen the birds do it every day. One day, when there was no one around, I decided to prove it once and for all! With the greatest self-confidence, I tied a towel around my neck (if it worked for Superman it would work for me, right?), climbed up to the top of the chicken house and checked once more to make sure there was no one lurking about. I calmly stepped to the edge of the roof and jumped. I waved my arms as fast as I could, but, alas, I plummeted to the ground. Fortunately, I did not seriously injure myself but I was in deep trouble with my mother. Even after that incident, I was still convinced that I could fly if I could just figure out how to flap my arms fast enough! Such is the unlimited thinking of a small child before we become indoctrinated with societal conditioning.

When I make a choice to do something that is difficult or considered by some to be impossible, I touch in with that tenacious child within me and I know that I can do it! As they say, "A difficult task will take a couple of days; an impossible task may take a little longer." Many wonderful things have been accomplished in this world by people who did not buy into the belief that it was impossible.

Part of the reason that I have not lived the life of my dreams in the past is that I let myself be separated from the healthy magical thinking of my childhood. I allowed my life to be ruled by what might be considered logical or reasonable. Sometimes it is just time to pull out our magical thinking and let it soar unrestricted. "Never tell a person that something can't be done. God may have been waiting for centuries for someone ignorant enough of the impossible to do that very thing." John Andrew Holmes

Embrace your beginner's mind, as our friends the Buddhists say, "Shoshin". Think about when you were three, four or five years old, or whatever age you were, when you still knew that you could do absolutely anything. What age were you before you started to believe what those around you were telling you about limitations? One caveat is, always use wisdom when touching into your magical thinking. By wisdom I do not mean logic. In fact, true wisdom may be what is telling us to do the illogical and the "impossible." *Wisdom is that part of our consciousness that tells us to proceed only if it aligns with our core values and is not intentionally hurting anyone or anything.* It is the "still, small voice" of the Divine.

Visualization

"If you think you can; if you think you can't, you're right." Henry Ford

In order to bring your heart's desire into manifestation, you must believe that you can. Even if there is only a tiny part of yourself that believes it, take that part and focus your attention on it. Focused attention acts like a magnifying glass; it will cause that tiny part of you that believes in yourself to become larger. Eric Butterworth wrote, "You don't so much get what you want, you get more of what you expect". Whatever you allow yourself to believe and expect is what you will bring about in your life. If you have thoughts, visions and expectations of being on the receiving end of your dreams they are much more likely to manifest in the world. If you feel defeated from within, the likelihood of your dreams coming to fruition will be slim until you change your thoughts. You must first get a clear picture of what you want. Use as many of your senses as possible to create a sharp picture in your mind. Use sight, sound, smell, taste and touch to make it real in your mind. The more of your senses you use to create the image the more powerful it will be. As you use your senses, also allow yourself to feel the excitement and gratitude that is inside you.

Intention + emotion + senses = manifestation.

If a new car is one of your heart's desires, embrace it. A new car can be a heart's desire that is placed there by God. A new car simply for the sake of a new car is not the goal. It is more about what good can come as a result of having the car. It can be used in many constructive ways that can be of great benefit. If it is simply something that you want in order to feed your lagging ego, you might want to take a closer look at it.

The process of visualization can be very beneficial in bringing your good into manifestation. Visualize, in your mind's eye, walking toward your new car. What make and model is it? What color is it? Feel the feelings of gratitude well up inside you because you get to have the use of this beautiful, comfortable, highly functional and dependable vehicle. As you approach the car and reach out, feel the handle in your hand as you open the door. Feel yourself lower your head to get into the driver's seat. Hear the door close. Once you are comfortable in the seat, you notice that the mirrors and the seat are in the perfect position for you. Smell that new car smell and feel the steering wheel in your hands. Take a moment, again, to focus on the emotions inside you. You are feeling excited, grateful and somewhat like a kid with a new toy. Maybe it has been a while since you allowed yourself the full extent of your feelings of excitement. Maybe you have been told that it is not the adult thing to do. Let go of that message. Sustain those feelings of gratitude and excitement for as long as you can. Emotion added to visualization will hasten results. Look around at the interior. What color are the seats? What color is the carpet? Where are the instruments located on the dash? Where are the radio and CD player? Where are the controls to the air conditioner? Reach for the key and feel it in your hand. Turn on the engine and hear the motor. What sound does it make? Back out of the driveway and onto the street. You are going to your favorite store so you see the familiar streets through the windshield. You turn into the parking lot, find a parking place and turn off the engine. You feel the handle in your hand as you open the car door. You get out of the car, close the door and lock it. You walk toward the store and pause to turn back and look at your new car one more time. The feeling of gratitude and excitement well up within you again and you say a silent prayer of thanks.

This exercise works with anything that is your heart's desire; a relationship, a house, a new outfit, a pet, a job, an attitude, health etc. You can use visualization to attract anything that you desire. Remember to use as many of your five senses as possible and it is very important to allow yourself to get excited. The use of the senses plus emotion will hasten your heart's desire into manifestation.

A very important piece is to examine what you intend to visualize and ask yourself: Is this for my highest good? Does it come to me with ease or is there financial struggle or unwise debt involved? Is it constructive? Is it for the good of all concerned?

Your mind does not know the difference between imagined and so called real situations and events. Your mind believes whatever you "feed" it. When you take time several times a day to visualize your heart's desire as a part of your life, especially if you use feelings and emotions along with pictures, the likelihood is very great that they will be manifest. Just as different seeds take different amounts of time to incubate before sprouting above ground; your heart's desires will take different times to manifest. Don't give up too soon!

A Wonderful, Unexpected Bonus

I had been single for a number of years and lived in a townhouse that I leased. I really liked my townhouse and the neighborhood in which I lived. My neighborhood had lots of trees and a small body of water that I passed when I went for my walks. I liked my neighbors and the landlords. I felt very content there. After many years of home ownership, previous to this time, it felt good to leave the maintenance, taxes and improvements to the care of someone else. It worked very well because it freed me up to spend more time in my position as minister in a wonderful church with loving, caring people. After being in the townhouse a few years, I began to miss having a backyard, dogs and more outdoor privacy so I started driving around in neighborhoods and checking out real estate websites to see what I might buy. When I had looked around a bit, I decided what I wanted and began to visualize it. In my visualization I saw myself driving home from my office and getting near my home. The street had large, old trees lining the sides and I could see children playing in some of the yards. It looked like a really friendly neighborhood, one in which I would like to live. I pictured myself turning into the driveway of a white brick house and pressing the garage door opener. The off-white garage door opened up and I drove into a one-car garage. It had plenty of room for my car and a few things that I stored there. I got out of my car and walked through the door into the sunlit kitchen with red curtains and red throw rugs on the floor. I then walked through the dining room that had a light colored wooden table and four chairs to match. To the right of the dining room was the living room with the sofa, two chairs and coffee table. I walked down the hallway to the bedrooms. My bedroom had an adjoining bathroom and there was a guest bath in the hall. There was a home office for me with a shiny wooden desk and several chairs at various places in the room. There was a guest bedroom with a queen-size bed, a dresser and my full length mirror on a stand. Most of the house had wheat colored carpet. I had a "knowing" that the numbers in the address of my new home would be a number one in numerology.

At various times during the day I would take time to close my eyes and visualize this house, just as I described and that it would come to me easily and without creating more debt for myself. In 2010 I moved into the house that I had been visualizing and little did I know that it came with a huge bonus – a kind and loving husband! (Good looking too!) I now live in the house that I visualized with most of the details exactly like I had been visualizing. I began the detailed visualization about 8 months before Danny and I even started dating. Danny is one of the most genuinely kind people that I have known. His "default position" is always kindness. At the time that I started visualizing myself in this house, I hadn't even had a date with him and certainly did not know the description of the house in which he lived. This is further proof that God has more good in store for us than we could even imagine. That is one of the reasons that I complete my prayers and visualizations with this phrase, "This or something even better for the good of all involved." We also adopted two rescue dogs, Freckles and Bo Bo. I got to live in the house that I had visualized and the "something better"!

When we get clear in our minds exactly what we want, it is much easier for the universe to bring us together with it. The invisible forces of the universe rise up to support our bravery, focus and commitment. Henry David Thoreau said it so well:

"If one advances confidently in the direction of his dreams and endeavors to live the life which he has imagined, he will meet with success unexpected in common hours. He will put something behind, will pass the invisible boundary; new universal and more liberal laws will begin to establish themselves around him or old laws will be expanded and interpreted in his favor in a more liberal sense and *he will live with the license of a higher order of beings!"*

I have a copy of this very encouraging quotation just above my computer where it is in my field of vision while I am doing my computer work. I feel a special affinity to it. Its words lift me up and help me to advance confidently in the direction of my dreams. I know that it is within me to accomplish *all* of my heart's desires; sometimes I just need to be reminded.

The Power of Thought

"The thinking faculty in you makes you a free agent, because it is your creative center; in and through this one power you establish your consciousness – you build your world." Charles Fillmore

Everything in our world that does not originate in nature was first a thought in the mind of a person. The chair upon which you sit was first a thought in a person's mind before it was a chair. The car you drive was once a thought in the mind of a person and now it is your transportation. Books were once rare and very expensive to produce until the idea of the printing press was conceived. Now you, and many like you, have this book in your hands. Everything that does not occur in nature was once a thought. Even those things that occur in nature were once a thought in the mind of God.

Not only do our thoughts create our lives and our world but we get to choose what we think. It may seem that thoughts in your mind are random, but that is not so. Our minds are like computers. A computer must have a program that contains specific information for us to get that information from it. The computer will only produce that which has been programmed into it. In that sense, our minds are like computers. Whatever we put into our minds is what we will get from our minds. "Beauty in; beauty out. Garbage in; garbage out." We are each responsible for most of what goes into our minds. We each have some measure of control as to what that will be. We can feed our minds on beauty or we can feed our minds on garbage. Of course there are varying degrees of each. If we expect to live the life of our dreams, we must put into our minds those ingredients which will help to build the life we want. We can choose to read, watch, and listen to positive, healthy and useful material or we can choose something different from that. If we don't make a conscious choice about what goes into our mind and we just let in random information, then what comes out will be random and unfocused. We are each a "free agent" as Charles Fillmore put it. It may seem simplistic and, on some level, it is. Again, some of life's greatest teachings are simple ones. In short, what goes into our minds is what comes out!

We would be using wisdom to, periodically, ask ourselves if our current activity is taking us in the direction of our dreams or is it taking us on a detour? In order to live a life that we love, some things are required of us. Focusing our mind on positive, constructive thoughts is definitely one of those things.

Incurable Optimist

There were two men, one named Sam and the other named Jed. Sam and Jed were determined to be rich. They had tried many schemes to get rich and, as of yet, had not found one that worked. One day they heard one of the local townspeople talking and found out that a live wolf would bring $10,000. They made their plan and set out the next day to hunt wolves. They hunted day and night for weeks and had not come up with a single wolf. They became discouraged and talked about giving up. One night, after hunting all day, they set up camp and fell asleep. In the night Sam woke up to find that they were surrounded by fifty wolves that were growling and showing their teeth. Sam poked his friend and yelled, "Wake up Jed, we're rich!"

If you looked up the term, "incurable optimist", I am sure Sam's picture would be there! In order to manifest our dreams, we would do well to get to the place of being called an incurable optimist by our friends and family. Isn't it interesting that the term, "incurable optimist," places optimism in the same category as a disease.

We move in the direction of our dreams when we allow only positive thoughts to take root in our mind. Thoughts are like seeds. When we have a positive thought and we allow it to fall on the fertile ground of our mind it germinates and grows into the beautiful flowers of our life. In the same way, when we have an unhealthy thought it is like a weed seed. Before the unhealthy thought has time to lie in the fertile soil of our minds, germinate and grow, we would do well to pluck it out. A seed is much easier to get rid of than a full grown plant with deep roots. In our lives, we will have both positive and negative around us. Fortunately, we are free agents and we get to choose what seed thoughts we will allow to germinate and grow.

If you have been in the habit of negative, unhealthy thinking for a very long time and set about to change it, do not be discouraged along the way. It can take some time to retrain your mind. I don't believe that we are born with negative thinking as one of our inborn traits. We learn how to think negative thoughts from those around us. Just as we learned to think negative thoughts, we can unlearn them. We can practice choosing positive affirming thoughts by setting our intention upon being aware when our thoughts move into the negative realm. Once we notice the negative thoughts, we can release them and replace them with more positive ones. Remember to simply release the negative thought, don't struggle with it or move into self-criticism. Whatever we give our energy to grows stronger in our life. Don't give over your precious energy to struggle and negativity.

For example:

If you think the thought, "Nothing ever goes my way," replace it with, "Everything goes my way." If you think the thought, "No one loves me," replace it with, "I am deeply loved by those around me." If you think the thought, "If it weren't for bad luck, I'd have no luck at all," replace it with, "I am a very fortunate person and I am grateful."

When I first started saying affirmations to change my negative thinking, I didn't believe a word of what I was saying. However, my life was such a disaster and I wanted so much to change it that I was willing to try just about anything. In the beginning, I was holding onto the teachings of a few people in whom I felt a measure of trust. One of the affirmations that eventually served to change my life in remarkable ways is this; "Everyone is always helpful." I got this affirmation from the book, *You Can Heal Your Life*, by Louise Hay. I felt like the direct opposite of this affirmation was true in my life. Even though that affirmation felt like a lie, I wanted it to be true, so I began saying it as often during the day as it occurred to me. After a while I began to notice that I was receiving help in areas that I had not anticipated. I continued to say that affirmation and it became true for my life. Many of the unsupportive people in my life either changed or fell away. I still use it today.

Vibrational Match

Beyond the obvious meaning of our thoughts is the fact that our thoughts create a vibration. That vibration then reaches out to find a perfect match. A negative thought will find a negative vibrational frequency to attract or be attracted to. By the same principle a positive thought will move out and find a positive vibrational match to attract. *Like attracts like.* We hear much about the Law of Attraction these days and the power of thought is a very good example of that principle. Change your thoughts; change your life. It is simple and true.

Just like thoughts, words help to create our lives. When we make statements, we are declaring to the universe that we want more of the contents of the statement. It does not matter whether the statement is positive or negative. *The universe supports whatever we choose to believe.* If we make the statement, "I am always broke," the universe moves in to support that statement by helping to create situations which make that statement true in the relative world.

In spirit, you can never be broke because there is unlimited substance from which to draw. If you affirm a statement such as the one by Charles Fillmore, "The inexhaustible Resource of Spirit is equal to every demand. There is no reality in lack. Abundance is here and now manifest;" you are aligning with the capital "T" Truth. We are fortunate in the way that a positive statement brings with it positive vibrations. The power of a positive thought is said, by some metaphysicians, to be at least 100 times more powerful than a negative thought. Negative vibrations are weaker and a much lower frequency. Meaning, *positive trumps negative every time!*

The written word helps to shape our lives. There is a powerful vibrational frequency in the written word. Each time that we read the words aloud, they imprint on our minds at an even deeper level and do double duty because we see them and hear them.

Treasure Mapping and Vision Boards

An activity with long, proven results is the creation of a Treasure Map or Vision Board. This is a process where we collect pictures of what we want for our lives and paste them on a poster board or on pages inside a folder. The pictures and words are usually cut out of magazines. Markers, stickers and colored pens may be used. Be creative! The poster is then placed where it can be seen daily, preferably, several times a day. The same process can be done with a folder and loose leaf pages. Folders are portable and great for traveling or for referring to often during the day.

Each time you look at these images they are placed in your mind in a fresh way and will help to bring them into the material world. When we use thoughts, written words, spoken words and images along with emotions it speeds up the process of manifestation.

Some years ago, I had a friend who wanted to move to Europe; specifically, Germany. She wanted to do more than just vacation there. She wanted to live there for at least a year or two and yet she had no idea how that could happen. When she looked at her finances and the circumstances of her life, it seemed like an impossible dream. She made a vision board with pictures of specific places that she wanted to visit. She placed this vision board in the back of her walk-in closet so that her dream was kept private and every time she opened the door it was the first thing that she saw. The vision board remained there for months with no apparent progress. She did not give up. She didn't get any big financial boon that could pay her way but, still, she did not give up. One day, while at work, she became aware of a job opening within her company, in – you guessed it – Germany! She immediately applied for the position knowing that many, many others were doing the same thing. After applying for the position, she stepped up her focus on her vision board making an effort to spend time with it every day. *She got the job!* She was able to live in Germany for the better part of two years and tour the rest of Europe on her days off. She was able to live out her dream and she got paid for it! The experience far exceeded her original expectations. She has since used vision boards to create other travel experiences that have come about in ways that she would never have expected. Vision boards work!

Our minds cannot tell the difference between a real event and an imagined one. Our faculty of imagination is one of our greatest, God given, tools to create a life that we love living!

What You See is What You Get

The once popular phrase, "What you see is what you get", stands true when you look at it from a metaphysical viewpoint. The use of the word "see" is that which you do with your imagination in your mind's eye. You must prepare the soil of your mind with all that it takes to make fertile ground so that the seeds that you have planted in your imagination will grow a crop of desired results.

God gives us many tools with which to build a life we love. A few of these tools are thought, the spoken word, the written word, and our imagination. When we receive these tools as the gift that they are intended to be and use them in accordance with spiritual principles, the result is a fuller, richer life!

What would you ask for today, if you were brave? Do not hesitate to ask for what you really want! Go boldly before the throne of God! Precious Child, it is God's good pleasure to give you the kingdom! Move *now* in the direction of your dreams! ***If not now, when?***

Affirmations

I am a precious child of God and I deserve all good.

My good comes to me "pressed down, shaken together and running over."

The Universe rises up to support me.

CHAPTER VI

Who Have You Come Here to Be?

"It takes courage to grow up and become who you really are."

E. E. Cummings

"Your two big, cosmic purposes are to experience yourself as Divinity and to express yourself as Divinity."

Janie Kelley

Will the Real "You" Please Stand Up?

Having been made in the image and likeness of God, your purpose for being here is to *experience* yourself as Divinity and then to *express* yourself as Divinity. You are a beautiful, wonderful child of God and you are how God expresses in this world. You are the eyes, ears, hands, and feet of God. You are called into *Living Full-Tilt* and to be all that you came here to be. What you have come here to be is magnificent!

Just under your big, cosmic purpose, you have a personal purpose. There is something that you can do in service to yourself and to the world that no one else can do quite like you. No matter who you are, you have a calling. There is a purpose for your being here on earth at this particular time, in this particular place and with these particular people around you.

Because of societal conditioning, we may think of a calling as being something lofty or prestigious. By the world's standards only a small percentage of people have a calling but we are not dealing with the rules and standards set by the world. *Who makes up these rules anyway?* (I ask this question often)

Some people are called to be out front and in the lead in professions upon which society places great value. Others are called to be in support roles that may seem of lesser importance in the world view. However, where would leaders be without followers? Leaders and followers/supporters are the same level of importance. We must have both for our world to function well.

If you think one job is more important than another, think what it would be like if there were no sanitation workers. What would you do with your household trash? Think about going into a restaurant and finding that there is no one to take your order. So, no more eating out! What would happen if your car broke down and there were no mechanics? What would happen if there was no one to check you out at the super market or department store? Do you see that we are all important? We are each an important piece of the universal puzzle. Just because society places a higher premium on some positions than others does not make it true. Simply because masses of people agree on an idea does not make it a fact.

We are each called to give our gift to the world; whatever that gift may be. In doing so, we are rewarded as well as those whom we serve. The reward in giving your gift is the satisfaction of doing what you have come here to do and the spiritual high which comes when we know that we are living our life's purpose.

What if our soul has input about who we will be before we are born into this life? What if, when we are in spirit form, we co-create, with God, the life that we will live when we come to Earth.

I can just see myself before I came to Earth. I was a little spirit just floating around and having a good time and one day God said, "When you go to earth what would you like to do?" I answered back, "I think that I would like to lift people up and encourage those who are depressed and have lost all hope. I want to remind them of who they really are. They are precious expressions of You, God. I want to help people who are living in abusive situations to know that they have worth and value and were not meant to live that way. They are meant to be loved and respected. I want to teach them that You have placed within them unwavering guidance and a Divine Spark along with everything that they will ever need to make their way in the world. All they are required to do is remove the blocks and allow it to pour forth. I want to teach people who live in poverty they are meant to live lives of opulence and plenty." And God said, "Wonderful! The best way to teach those things is to experience what they are experiencing so that you can speak to them in a way that they can truly hear. They will understand you because you will have the compassion that comes from having been where they are." And, "poof," I was born!

Maybe it happens that way, maybe not. We each have our beliefs but no one really knows for sure.

Recognizing Your Life's Purpose

Where are you when it comes to recognizing your life's purpose?

1. Maybe you are already living on purpose and you know it.
2. Maybe you think you are living on purpose but you are not sure.
3. Maybe you think you *might* know your life's purpose but you are not currently living it.
4. Maybe you don't know your life's purpose.
5. Maybe you don't have a clue what "life's purpose" even means but you feel a deep unrest in your life and you just know there is something more.

For number one, I say, *Great, Rock On!*

For numbers two through five, the rest of this chapter will probably have special meaning for you.

Imagine this:

You are robustly healthy. You have plenty of energy to do all of the things that are of interest to you. You are so healthy that your friends and family remark about it from time to time. Your relationship with God is on a moment by moment basis and you feel centered in Spirit most, if not all, of the time. You have all of the education your heart desires up to this point. You are trained in all areas that are of interest to you and you are considered an expert in many of these fields. You are greatly admired. Your relationships are outstanding! Harmony seems to follow you wherever you go. You feel deeply loved. You express love freely. You have all of the money you could ever spend and it will last far beyond your lifetime. You know your money is secure and it is never an issue for you. You know that you will never have to work a day in your life unless you choose to do so. You are wise beyond your years. You make decisions which continue to enhance your life.

Since you don't have to work there isn't necessarily a job to report to each day. You don't have to do anything to make more money. You have all of the education that you want so you do not have to go to school. Your health is excellent so no time or energy is spent dealing with illness. Everything in your life is in place and working smoothly. When you wake up in the mornings, you are completely rested with energy to do whatever you want. Every area of your life is flowing well! Life is good! There is absolutely nothing that you *must* do.

You still have twenty-four hours in every day. You still have a full day, every day, to fill with activity of some kind. What would you do? How would you spend the hours in your day? In your mind's eye allow yourself to go through the activities of a full day. When you get out of bed and your feet touch the floor, what do you do first? You may skip over the mundane activities like brushing your teeth and combing your hair. What would be the first thing you would do? Would you take on some artistic endeavor? Would you call friends or family and make a date to see them? Would you tend your yard or garden? Would you volunteer at the local women's shelter or do some other work you believe in? Would you play an instrument? Would you travel to a developing country and help build schools? Would you volunteer at an animal shelter? What would make you really happy, long term? What would make you want to jump out of bed and get started immediately? What would make your heart sing? What activities could you look back on at the days end and know that the day was spent exactly the way you wanted? What would give you a deep sense of satisfaction?

Chances are great that the answers to these questions will give you a clue to your life's purpose. You have within yourself some basic heart's desires. Your answers could come right away like a light bulb going on in your head. You know what you would do and you feel excitement about doing it! You feel your heart singing a song at the mere thought of having that much freedom to do what you are drawn to do!

If you didn't know the answers to these questions right away, you have lots of company. Of the people I see in counseling, many have a measure of dissatisfaction with what they are currently doing as a career or life activities. Some even say they hate their work.

There is something or some things that tug at your heart and gently pull you in the direction of your life's purpose. When they go unfulfilled, they create a longing and discontent. Quite possibly, they have been long forgotten because you haven't thought about them in so long. You started out your life trying to please your parents or primary caregivers and that is natural. As a small child, they were your whole world and held your very survival in their hands. As you grew, you expanded that behavior to please your friends, teachers, co-workers, your boss, a spouse or partner, etc. We do this naturally because we want to fit in and be accepted and loved by the people in our world. It is not that we don't have ideas and dreams of our own. It is that sometimes we trade our own dreams for someone else's dream for us. We want to be accepted, we want to be loved, and we don't want to disappoint those people who are important in our lives. Maybe you can't remember exactly when it happened because there was nothing special that marked the folding up and putting away of your dream and the opening up of someone's dream for you. Or maybe it was more overt and you felt pressured, so you traded your own dream for the dream of another.

You may have allowed the negative input from others to convince you that your dream was impractical, unlikely or downright impossible. Maybe someone told you all of the reasons that it would not work and simply was not a good idea and you believed them. You may have even been teased or ridiculed about your dream. There are many times in our lives that we are vulnerable and easily convinced of another person's point of view.

For the most part, people in your life probably thought that they were giving you the best advice possible. Maybe they thought that they were saving you from being hurt or disappointed. Most, if not all, of those people probably loved you. There is really no one to blame. And, even if there was, blaming in any form is destructive. It is a form of unforgiveness. Blame can be directed toward others in your life or it can be directed inward toward yourself. Either way, it is still destructive. If you are holding blame for anyone, it is eating up your creative energy and prevents you from reaching your full potential. Do your forgiveness work around anyone for whom you still feel any blame. Free yourself of this weight and allow yourself to fly free! They were doing the best they knew how to do given the amount of information and experience that they had at the time. If you talked to them today they would likely give you very different advice. You would do well to forgive and release *all* blame. Blame only saps the energy of today and keeps us ineffective in what we are intending to accomplish.

The Wisdom of an Eighteen year old

Would you want an eighteen year-old telling you what to do with your life? No? For most of us that is exactly what happened! When we were about eighteen we made major, life-changing decisions about who and what we would be. Many of our choices may have seemed right at the time and maybe they served us well for a period. Or, maybe our choices never really served us in a satisfying way but for reasons that seemed important, we just never made any changes. It is never too late to look at our heart's desires and make the necessary changes that will move us in the direction of our dreams. Let yourself off the hook! You made the best decisions that you knew how to make at eighteen given the information and experience you had at the time.

In the life that you imagined earlier where everything was taken care of, if you could not decide what you would do, try this exercise:

Take some time alone and allow your mind to go back to your first memories of being a child. What did you like to do with your time? When you thought about being a grownup, what kinds of things did you see yourself doing? Did you have hobbies that you really enjoyed? What were your daydreams? Continue to ask yourself these and any other helpful questions about your early life. Don't just think about it, allow yourself to be the child again. Choose to take some time to lose yourself in being that child again. Chances are great that you will connect with some clues as to who you came here to be. It may be such a departure from where you are that it takes a while for the images to come up. Hang in there! Don't give up! The rewards will be worth your effort! Living out your life's purpose is rewarding and satisfying in a way that nothing else can touch.

Be gentle with yourself if the answers are not forthcoming. It may take a while for the pattern to emerge, especially if you have been disconnected from your original dreams for some time. You may need help from a trusted friend, counselor, or minister. Allow yourself whatever you need to let the pattern surface.

Knowing your deepest heart's desires is the first step to putting into practice your life's purpose. You cannot make your heart's desires a part of your life until you know what they are.

Living your life's purpose can mean the difference between trudging through life just marking time, barely getting by and living, really living, a life of purpose and deep satisfaction.

Once you find out who you have come here to be, it may mean that you continue to do what you are currently doing because you have found that they are a match. It may mean that you need to do some tweaking but the basics remain the same. It may mean some uncomfortable changes must take place in order for you to fulfill your life's purpose. It may mean a whole new life. Regardless of how you are affected; "It takes courage to grow up and become who you really are." E. E. Cummings

Act As If

What would you do if you were living the life of your dreams? How would you dress? How would you act? Where would you spend your time and money? Get dressed in the clothes that you already own that make you feel the wealthiest. Wear clothes that help you to feel like you are living your calling. Maybe the clothes that would help you to feel wealthy are classic and tailored. Maybe they are sparkly and have a lot of "bling". Maybe the clothes that help you to feel the wealthiest are very ordinary looking and you believe that when you are really wealthy you will dress in a way that shows that you have nothing to prove. Once you are dressed, go out to a store that is a grade above the store where you usually shop. As you walk in observe how you feel. Observe without judgment. Look around the store and allow yourself to know that you are a precious expression of God and you deserve all good. Look at the merchandise, feel it, hold it in your hand, try it on and know that this merchandise is for you. Buy something from this store and place it where it can be easily seen in your home, or workplace. Each time you look at it you will be reminded that the Truth of you is that you have access to the unlimited good of the Universe.

Go to a restaurant that is more upscale than the usual places you go to eat out. Look at the surroundings. Observe how you feel as you look at the décor. Just observe without judgment. When you are seated, order something from the menu. It may be only an appetizer and a drink or dessert and coffee. Just know that soon you will be eating full meals at this restaurant easily and regularly, if you so choose. Allow yourself to take in all of the upscale beauty around you. Unleash your senses! Know that the opportunity to live at this level is here for you and within your reach. Know that you deserve this and even more.

Go to the best hotel in town, one with live music or a piano bar, if that is available. Being in an upscale environment where there is live music just feels rich. Maybe order a drink and listen to the music for a while, all the time telling yourself that you deserve to live enjoying some of life's richest treasures.

Do these things, and anything else, that comes to your mind at the level that you can manage at this time knowing that it is only a matter of time until you will be frequenting these places because of your new more opulent way of living. Do these things as often as possible to get comfortable with your better way of living. Saturate yourself with "the good life." By doing so, you will not only be living more gracefully but you will become a beacon of light for those around you. Your better standard of living will silently give others permission to live a better life; maybe even the life of their dreams. When we all influence each other to live the life of our dreams, can you even imagine the harmony and peace that will emanate around the world!

Having a better standard of living is only a part of *Living Full-Tilt*. There are many facets to living the life we are intended to live. We are here to know who we really are and live our life from that knowledge.

What would you do if you already were the person you have come here to be? How would you act? What things would you do that are different than what you are doing now? Start now doing those things! Know that the person that you have come here to be is inside you and has never been away from you. You may not have been in touch with this person in a while but that doesn't mean the real you has gone anywhere.

As much as you can, right now, begin to be the person you most aspire to be. If your dream life is to be a singer, start now singing every chance you get. Even if you are not ready for the public – sing! Sing in the car, your house, the shower, anywhere that you feel comfortable; just sing! If you want to be a public speaker start speaking in front of your mirror or at small gatherings. If you want to own your own business, write out a business plan and look at properties.

In order to make these changes, much of the time, you must go beyond the limiting perceptions that you have of yourself and step into the role of the person you came here to be. You are likely to be in a position to use your courage. There may be changes that require all of the courage you can muster up. Remember this; along with your heart's desires comes everything you will ever need to fulfill those desires. Your heart's desires and your life's purpose are connected. You have within you every single thing you will ever need.

Powerful Beyond Measure

"Our deepest fear is not that we are inadequate. Our deepest fear is that we are powerful beyond measure. It is our light, not our darkness, that most frightens us. We ask ourselves, 'Who am I to be brilliant, gorgeous, talented, fabulous?' Actually, who are you not to be? You are a child of God. Your playing small does not serve the world. There is nothing enlightened about shrinking so that others won't feel insecure around you. We are all meant to shine as children do. We were born to make manifest the Glory of God that is within us. It is not in some, it is in everyone. As we let our light shine, we unconsciously give other people permission to do the same. As we are liberated from our own fear, our presence automatically liberates others." Marianne Williamson

When we make changes in our life and we begin to live the life of our dreams, it will give some other people permission to do the same. It may also have a different effect on some others. Some will see the joy in our life and want that for themselves and yet not know how to achieve it. For some, it may bring up jealousy, criticism and envy. They may try to get you to return to your former, limited self so that they can feel okay about themselves. Be patient with them as far as you can but don't let them rob you of your dream.

Bill decided to go crabbing and take Brandon, his grandson. This would be Brandon's first crabbing trip. They got together everything necessary for this day's excursion, the bait, string, dip-net and a large bucket to hold the crabs. Bill took Brandon to his "lucky crabbing spot" because he wanted Brandon to have a great experience. They got settled, put the bait on the string then into the water. Right away, there was a tug at Brandon's string and Bill got the net and pulled the crab to the surface. Brandon was so happy that he had caught his first crab. Bill placed it in the bucket and put the lid on top. Almost immediately Bill caught a crab and Brandon caught another one. Bill placed them in the large bucket but this time he did not place the lid on top. Brandon was worried that the crabs might escape, so he said to his grandpa, "Put the lid on top before they get away." Bill said, "They won't get away. Just watch them for a while." Brandon sat and watched as one of the crabs made its way up the side of the bucket. Just as it was about to reach the top the other crabs reached up and pulled it back down into the bucket. Brandon said, "I see what you mean, Grandpa". Crabs will continue to pull each other down until they just give up. We can gain wonderful insights by observing nature.

This is sometimes the way it is with people around us. If you accomplish the life of your dreams, or even make steps in that direction, it may feel threatening to other people in your life. In order for them to feel okay with their own lives they will try to get you back down "into the bucket" so that they can once again feel comfortable. They may want to step into the flow of life the way that you have and yet maybe they are not in touch with their courage and ability to move forward with these urges. Maybe they lack the knowledge and skills. Sometimes, people criticize and discourage because they think that they are saving you from pain and failure. Whatever is the reason that they criticize, belittle or minimize your success and forward movement in life, just know that they will either, eventually come around and be happy with you or there may be a falling away. People are in our lives "for a reason, a season or a lifetime."

You have the ability to reach your full potential. It may take courage that you did not know you had. Philosopher James Allen said, *"Through his thoughts man holds the key to every situation and contains within himself that transforming and regenerative agency by which he may make himself what he will."*

You hold the key to your own transformation. You have the God-given ability to be anything you truly want to be. You must be willing to follow your inner, spiritual guidance and use all that is available to you.

Affirmations

I am made in the image and likeness of God.

I am perfect, whole and complete; lacking in nothing.

I am enough.

CHAPTER VII

Commitment is Required

"Whatever you can or dream you can do, begin it. Boldness has power and genius in it."

Goethe

"The way that we know that we are 100% committed is that there is no 'Plan B'."

Janie Kelley

Set Your Mind

Commitment is a very important key to transformation. Regardless of what we learn from teachers, books, seminars and workshops, we must be committed to doing whatever it takes until we see results! Without commitment, reading this book or attending my workshop is simply a fun way to spend a day or two. The principles, concepts and ideas that you learn will have little or no lasting effect without commitment. No amount of head knowledge can take the place of full-out determination and commitment. To go the distance we must set our mind to take the steps that make change possible. We must remain committed until we achieve the results we seek or, until we are guided to a different goal.

Napoleon Hill, author of *Think and Grow Rich,* wrote, "More than 500 of the most successful men this country has ever known told the author that their greatest success came just one step *beyond* the point at which defeat had overtaken them."

The most valuable life lesson I learned from my mom is a simple statement that she used to say to me often, "Janie, you can do anything you set your mind to." She instilled that statement in me at the very deepest level for which I will be eternally grateful. I heard it from her so often that it became a part of who I am. It has helped me through some of my life's roughest, darkest places. The knowing that I could "do anything I set my mind to" has been one of my life's saving graces. It has also taken me to my life's highest achievements. There have been many times in my life I used this lesson without really sitting down and saying to myself, "I can do anything I set my mind to." Because it was so deeply ingrained in me, I just acted from the knowing that it was true.

A few years ago I went to the Master Prosperity Teacher Training given by Edwene Gaines. This time it was one of those, "If they can do it I can do it," moments. I had wanted to take this training since the first time I saw Edwene Gaines in person some years before. She began the workshop by saying, "My name is Edwene Gaines and what I want you to know about me is I am a woman of power!" She had me right then! The *real me* identified with that statement. Having been a young woman in a rural area and in an era when women had very limited choices in life, I knew right away that I wanted what she had.

She is a wonderful prosperity teacher and coach and is incredibly funny while imparting valuable information and insight. Despite the culture in which I grew up, I have always leaned toward self-reliance and independence. During the workshop she said she was enlisting the help of co-equal laborers in the task of raising the prosperity consciousness of planet Earth. I knew in my heart I was one of those laborers and yet, I did not sign up for her training. I let fear stand in the way of moving forward on that important part of my calling. I was afraid that I could not teach effectively about prosperity in front of people. I had thoughts like, "Where would I get the money for the training? How would I work the training into my already too-full schedule? How could I speak in public?" (This was before I became a minister) You know how your fear will rise up to tell you all of the reasons why your heart's desire is silly, illogical, impractical, too hard, unacceptable, too expensive, time consuming, ludicrous, obscure and just plain won't work? My fear has a great vocabulary!

I would go on to see Edwene Gaines many more times over the following years; each time knowing that taking her training and doing prosperity work was mine to do. It is an important part of who I have come here to be. I bought all of her recordings, cards and support material. I bought her book, *The Four Spiritual Laws of Prosperity,* as soon as it came out. The years passed and I still would not allow myself to commit to take her training.

In 2010, I got an email offering enrollment in her Master Prosperity Teacher Training and immediately I thought, "I would love to do that!" In probably less than two minutes my fear rose up once again with its large vocabulary. It was telling me the usual story which sounded like this: "I don't have the time in my busy schedule to go. Besides, it is expensive and it's not a good time to take that on. Who will speak in my place on Sunday morning? How am I going to do one more thing", and so on and so on. Then my thoughts were interrupted with the "still, small voice" which I recognize so well. God speaks to me in thoughts that are not my own. These thoughts come to me in an instant "knowing" without words. The words come later in the fewest words possible and always straight to the point. The "voice" said *"If not now, when?"* Years had passed since I had attended my first workshop with Edwene Gaines in Houston, Texas. I knew, in the first moments of seeing her, this was mine to do. How much longer would I put it off? Would I continue to make excuses until the opportunity was gone? I understand that one of the most common end-of-life regrets is missed opportunities. Even though I did not know how I would do it, I made a commitment to move forward on the dream that I had harbored for years. I called the phone number and arranged for my non-refundable deposit. I made airline and hotel reservations. There was no looking back.

The whole experience cost the equivalent of about two months' salary. I made a commitment and asked God to have the money show up outside of my regular income. That was basically it. Every time I thought about it, I would not allow myself to entertain a Plan B. Extra money started to come in over about a three month period. Even though I had told no one about how I had asked God to provide the funds, about one week before it was time for me to leave, I was still a little over $1,000 short of my estimated expense. I had prayed and made a commitment that I was going to take the training, regardless of whether the money came in over and above my regular salary or not. I felt that it would be further confirmation that I was doing the right thing if the money came in the way I had asked. Less than a week before I was to leave a dear friend came into my office and handed me a check in the amount of $1,500. It was a tithe on an inheritance that she had received and she said that it was important to her that the tithe should go directly to me. This was the amount I needed plus an additional amount for fun money. This was like God saying to me, "Here is all that you asked and more."

Taking that training was one of the high points of my life. It has furthered my confidence in myself and moved me in the direction of my dreams. The workshop was informative, enriching, sacred, heart opening, mind stretching and loads of fun all at the same time.

Toward the end of the training, we were given the opportunity to do a fire walk. I had heard Edwene talk about this activity at a previous workshop and at first I said to myself, "Who would want to do that?" The truth is that I was full of fear about the fire. Once I understood that defying physical law and walking on red hot coals would help me to release fear and help eliminate belief in limitation, the thought of doing it became much more attractive. It was one of those situations where I said to myself, "If they can do it, I can do it." And I did. I walked on hot coals and did not have the slightest sign of a burn. It was amazing! The fire walk taught me several things. One of the most important lessons is this, *If I can defy physical law, I can do anything*! I have even more confidence in my ability to "do anything that I set my mind to," just like my mom taught me.

Commitment is what keeps us going when our best efforts seem to be failing. Just because we learn about higher Truths does not mean that there will not be difficulty and challenges. Jesus said, "In this world you will have tribulation." It would be hard to be clearer than that. And he went on to say, "… but be of good cheer for I have overcome the world." Jesus also said that we can do the same works that he did and even greater works. That means if Jesus was able to overcome the tribulations of the world, then we can too. We simply have to reach inside ourselves to that Divinity within. We are Points of Light Within the Greater Light! We are Precious Expressions of The Creator. It is written in both the Hebrew Scriptures (Old Testament, Psalm 82:6 WEB) and the Christian Scriptures (New Testament John 10:34 WEB), "You are gods." The same concept is taught in many of the world's religions. It is time for us, as a human race, to claim our heritage. The time has come for us to step up and take our rightful place. It is time to let our light shine!

Commitment is required to reach your highest potential. Half measures yield half results. You can make a commitment to move in the direction of your dreams and be co-creators with God for your life **or** you can live your life by default. When you co-create with God for your life, you get to move in the direction of your heart's desires.

Spirit is constantly encouraging us to move in the direction of our dreams. If we choose to live life by default, we will probably revert back to lower vibrational thinking, speaking and doing. There is no such thing as standing still. If we are not moving forward, we are losing ground.

Listens and Follows Directions

When I was a kid in elementary school I received a Report Card that I was to take home to my parents. They would look at my grades, sign it and I would take it back to my teacher as proof that my parents had seen my grades. On the left side of this Report Card were the academic subjects with a corresponding grade. On the right side of the Report Card there was a list entitled Conduct. Under the Conduct heading there were categories such as; "Plays Well With Others", "Finishes Work on Time" and "Shows Initiative". There was also a very important column in this list, "Listens and Follows Directions". I think of this often when I think of my role as an expression of The Divine. I sometimes wonder if God was to give me a Report Card today would I get a check mark in the column, "Listens and Follows Directions?"

Our spiritual guidance is always active and always present. There is never a split-second that we are without guidance from our Loving Creator. There may be times that we are not in tune with it, but it is always with us. Radio waves are always in the atmosphere, but we won't hear them until we tune in with a receiver. What we hear over the receiver depends on the frequency to which we are tuned. Spiritually speaking, we must have an open receiver (heart and mind) and it must be tuned on the correct frequency (the voice of Spirit).

When we make commitments in the direction of our dreams, everything unlike those commitments comes up to be healed. Just know that changes will happen and the changes bring us closer to the life of our dreams.

It takes commitment to:

- Acknowledge your deservability and prepare yourself to receive.
- Forgive everyone, of everything, all of the time, especially yourself, no exceptions.
- Choose to live in a constant, over-arching state of gratitude.
- Tithe and give back in order to continue to prosper.
- Set goals and carry them out or make a conscious choice to change them.
- Find and live your Divine Purpose.

In order to be of maximum effectiveness, 100% commitment is needed. That is not to say that we will hit the target every time, but with 100% commitment we will keep moving in a forward direction with our eye on the prize.

We take the steps necessary to live the life of our dreams knowing that each step takes us closer and closer to the goal; even the ones that may appear to be mistakes. It is very important to begin with the end in mind. We keep the end in mind just as one who is swimming to a shore keeps his eyes on a landmark. Each stroke of the swim is very important and each stroke counts as the swimmer makes way to dry land.

No Plan "B"

The way that you know that you are 100% committed is that there is no Plan B.

In 1982 I opened a ladies clothing and accessories boutique. In 1983 I bought the hair salon in which I worked making me the owner of two businesses. In January of 1984 I got divorced.

If you know anything about small businesses, you know that it generally takes a few years to get established before the business begins to make a profit. I didn't know that when I opened my businesses. I was married at the time and thought that I did not need to make my living totally from my businesses. That all changed with the divorce. I had children, a mortgage, and upkeep on my home, a car note, utilities, food and all of the regular life expenses, with no child support. I had to make a living out of my businesses. There was no Plan B. There were some very lean times, to say the least. There were several times that I came close to foreclosure on my home but somehow always managed to pull out of it. I owned my businesses, simultaneously, for 23 years as my major means of support. I never entertained a Plan B. It was not so much that I sat down one day and wrote out a commitment statement declaring that I had no Plan B. Even though that is an excellent practice and would have been valuable, I didn't know to do it at that time. Over the course of my life, Spirit has helped me through similar situations when *I didn't know what I didn't know.* If I had known, in advance, some of the difficulties that I would face, I probably would not have ventured into those businesses, especially owning two at a time. If that had been the case, I would have missed out on some of the richest, most teaching and rewarding experiences of my life. I would have missed the loving, adventurous, growth-producing and sometimes strained relationships that I had with clients and employees as a result of owning those businesses. I would probably have missed out on working for the professional hair product companies (in the 1990's and early 2000's) which afforded me education and travel to places I may have never seen. Prior to working for these companies my life ran in a fairly tight little circle. Fear kept me from venturing out very far. It was on my first, company paid, trip that I got to go to Los Angeles for the first time, and it was there that I got to have sushi for the first time. At that time, getting to go to California was a really big deal! Eating sushi for the first time was a really big deal. As I moved up in the company, I got to spend a week at a very upscale resort in Scottsdale, Arizona; all expenses paid. On another trip to California I got to shop on Rodeo Drive in Beverly Hills; again at company expense. I got to do stage work at hair shows with hundreds of people in the attendance in cities that I might otherwise have never seen. And, the list goes on. It was a twenty-three year adventure.

As I look back on those years, the difficult places moved me forward into growth that I may have never experienced had I played it safe. I am not writing this as a means of setting myself apart from anyone but, instead, to let you know that I am no stranger to what one might call the real world of highs and lows and to let you know what can be accomplished with commitment. I also know that in every adversity there are gifts of equal proportions available to me. My life is proof of it.

Somewhere in the mid-eighties I hit bottom. Everything about my life changed. I was single after being married most of my adult life. I got married very young and had no idea, really, how to be single. I owned businesses for which I had little or no preparation or prior experience and these businesses were my only means of support. My children were in early adulthood and began to move out, as young adults do.

I found Unity and after attending for a while, I began to "get it" that I have the power to influence my life for the better through my thoughts, words and actions. My commitment now is to teach others what I have learned and am still learning. There is an Eastern proverb that states, "Teach what you would learn". I will be the first to tell you that I still have much to learn. I am committed to learning right along with you by teaching the concepts and principles which I wish to know at a deeper level.

"Until one is committed, there is hesitancy, the chance to draw back - Concerning all acts of initiative (and creation) there is one elementary truth that ignorance of which kills countless ideas and splendid plans; that the moment one definitely commits oneself then providence moves too. All sorts of things occur to help one that never would have otherwise occurred. A whole stream of events issues from the decision raising in one's favor all manner of unforeseen incidents and meetings and material assistance which no man could have dreamed would come his way. Whatever you can or dream you can do begin it. Boldness has genius, power and magic in it. Begin it now." Goethe

"The moment one definitely commits oneself then Providence moves too". When we are 100% committed the Universe rises up to support us.

The Tipping Point

Malcolm Gladwell, the author of *The Tipping Point, How Little Things Can Make a Big Difference*, defines the tipping point this way, "the moment of critical mass, the threshold, the boiling point." It is that subtle point at which everything changes. We can put a pot of water on the stove and turn on the heat. It will simply be hot water until it reaches that moment when it gets to the 212 degree-point and begins to boil and the water changes form and becomes steam. That is the tipping point. Before 212 degrees it was simply a pot of hot water. It is the same when it comes to that point in our lives that we have made a firm commitment to do a certain thing. At the tipping point, the magic moment, all sorts of unseen forces are set into action.

As Goethe pointed out, commitment requires a degree of boldness. The degree of boldness depends upon how life changing the commitment may be. It would take a certain amount of boldness to commit to having a dinner party for 50 guests. It would take a greater boldness to quit one's safe job of long standing and move to a different city to pursue one's dream of being an artist. Notice I said that it takes a different level of boldness and not a different level of commitment. True commitment is the same no matter what one is committing to. There are levels of boldness but one is either committed or not.

The universe honors that to which we give our focus and energy. By making a commitment we have made a decision to place our focus on our goal and to do whatever it takes to achieve it. The spoken word is very powerful. The written word is very powerful. When making an important commitment, it is best to write out the commitment and be very clear about it. Once we have it written, we make it even more powerful by speaking the words out loud on a regular basis. If you are going to speak the words to another person, it is best to choose someone that is at the level of consciousness that will receive it and hold it with you. Use discernment when choosing such a person. Make sure that this person will be happy and celebrate with you when you fulfill your commitment. Also, choose a person in whom you trust for confidentiality.

You may not want the commitment that you have made to be public knowledge just yet. Or, you may not want it to be public knowledge at all. Choose wisely with whom you will share your dream.

For best results, read and speak your commitment at least twice a day, every day. Show the universe that you mean business!

Solitude and "Filling Your Glass"

Time with your self is very important. We live in a busy, noisy world and finding time to be in solitude is essential. There must be balance in our lives if we are to live the life of our dreams. The phrase, "Living Full-Tilt," may sound like we would be moving and doing constantly but that would be out of balance. In order to live a full life, you must take time to examine your life; take time to reflect and just "be".

The "doing" of life can be great fun and exciting! The doing must be counter-balanced with "non-doing." In the doing, it looks like more is accomplished than in the non-doing. However, we must have periods of rest where nothing is expected of us. No one can continue to function well under constant demands and expectations. There must be time to rest and replenish.

Ideally, you would have a whole day out of every week that nothing is expected of you; a day of relaxation and renewal. If you are constantly in the mode of doing and, more specifically, doing what is expected of you, it leaves no time to be creative.

In our various roles there are certain expectations. Doing what is expected can come from inside, as well. Be mindful of the demands and expectations that you may be placing on yourself, as well as, those that you allow to be placed on you by others. I don't mean this as being a victim but there are certain healthy expectations as a parent, employee, friend, a spouse or partner. We all have these. We would do well to be clear about both types.

Think of yourself as a glass of water. Think of those people in your life as straws. With your permission each person dips in his or her straw and draws out some water. A person can only draw from you with your permission. That permission may be a conscious or unconscious. If the glass (you) is not refilled at some point, eventually it will be empty and there is nothing left for you or the people in your life. We must "refill our glass" and do it on a regular basis.

Solitude can help refill the glass. Allow yourself to spend as much time as you need in solitude. The amount of time needed varies from person to person. Experiment and find what works well for you.

What is it that fills your glass? What is an activity that, when you do it, you feel energized physically, emotionally, mentally and spiritually? Is it reading, writing or going to the library? Going for long walks either alone or with someone? Is it sewing? Is it painting or some other form of art? Maybe it is giving dinner parties surrounded by friends. If you are often gone from home in your work, filling your glass may be simply staying at home and puttering around the house. What is it that "fills your glass?"

Some of the things which "fill my glass" are:

- Just looking around in furniture stores with no real intention of buying. I like to see the room arrangements and I redecorate my house in my mind.
- Leisure reading that has nothing to do with my vocation. I really like to get a magazine and read it cover to cover. I rarely get to read magazines, so this really feels like one of life's little luxuries.
- Walking in natural settings.
- Oil painting and drawing. I get completely immersed in the piece.
- Silent retreats of several days
- Lying in my hammock and reading or just looking at the sky
- Closing my eyes while I listen to the sounds of birds, dogs barking or neighbors in the distance.

Introvert/Extrovert

Extroverts get their energy from being with people. Conversation and just being with other people helps to "recharge their batteries"; so to speak. This does not mean that they do not need solitude because every healthy person needs time to reflect. Extraverts usually look for group activities to "fill their glasses." Extroverts may go out alone but that is usually not their first choice. Once they reach their destination, they usually are surrounded by people in a short period of time.

Introverts get their energy from being alone. Solitary activities help to recharge an introvert. Sometimes the word "introvert" is mistaken as being synonymous with hermit, yet they are not the same. An introvert may enjoy time spent with other people yet is recharged from solitary activities. A hermit usually chooses to live alone and away from social contact because, for whatever reason, he/she chooses not to be in the company of people. Being an introvert myself, I have first-hand information. If you will notice, all of my activities which fill my glass are solitary activities. I enjoy my time with people very much *and* I recharge from being alone.

The Universe Rises Up to Support You

Here is something I know, beyond a shadow of a doubt, if you make a 100 % commitment toward a goal, the Universe will rise up to support you! You will see doors open that you would have thought were closed to you. You will see people cooperate with you in ways you never imagined. There will be opportunities that look like miracles! The synchronicities will amaze you! Just the right person will appear exactly when you need them! You will find support comes to you from every direction. Sometimes it will seem like magic! With the Universe backing you and with your 100 % commitment; you will reach your goal!

Affirmations

I am worthy of making commitments to myself.

I take my commitments seriously and know that I am capable.

I can be trusted to keep my commitments.

CHAPTER VIII

Changes

"The only thing that remains the same is change".
Heraclitus

"Life is a series of changes."
Janie Kelley

Life Flows

With or without your cooperation, change happens. Nothing remains the same. Heraclitus is also quoted as having said, *"You cannot step into the same river twice."* Life flows like a river and there will never be a moment exactly like this one… or this one…or this one. Every moment of life is a change. The only question is the degree of change.

You can either be a co-creator with God for your life and move in the direction of our heart's desires or you can live your life by default and let life happen to you based on your old paradigm. When you live your life by default, you revert back to old patterns and behaviors. This may be just fine if the old patterns gave you desired results. If they did not, does it make sense to live by default?

Change is one of life's really important truths. When we get that concept, really get it, we have the potential of saving ourselves a lot of grief and difficulty. We cannot force life to stay the same nor can we go back to a "better" time. When we understand this truth, our relationship with life becomes a much gentler flow.

An important teaching in Buddhism is "The Impermanence of Everything". All things, as we know it, here on Earth will change. Nothing will stay the same. When we allow ourselves to develop an unhealthy attachment to people and circumstances suffering will result. People and circumstances always change or disappear. When we have a deep inner knowing that change is going to take place, it is much easier to hold people, objects and situations lightly, without grasping.

As human beings we have a tendency to resist change to some degree. There is a certain amount of comfort in the familiar, even if we are not satisfied with it. Sometimes we stay in situations long after there is any pleasure or satisfaction in doing so. The familiar can give us a false sense of security that we may not be willing to give up.

God is always with you. God is always within you. Whether or not you know it or feel it does not change it. In Buddhism it is called the "Buddha Nature." In Hinduism it is called "Atman". In Christianity it is called "Holy Spirit". Whatever you choose to call it, I invite you to listen to the God of your understanding and follow the still, small voice within you that helps you choose the best direction to take. Know that God will never leave you or forsake you. God is closer than your breath. Really, we do not breathe on our own; we are being breathed by the Universal Intelligence. Breathing is very basic to our survival and yet you do not breathe consciously most of the time. When you are asleep, how do you know to breathe? You are being breathed by the same Creative Force that made you. The essence that is God is always within you; it is always you.

Resisting change will not stop it. It is a waste of time and effort to try and stop change. Work with change to bring about the life that you love living. One way to go about it is to learn not only to release the resistance to change but to learn to embrace it. Learn to look at change as you would look at a friend. Welcome it.

"Chemicalization"

Do not be concerned about any symptoms which may arise as you make changes or plow with the changes in your life. The deeper the changes, the more likely you are to experience physical and/or emotional symptoms. Even if you have consciously chosen the changes that are occurring in your life, symptoms may arise. These symptoms are temporary. In her book, *Lessons in Truth,* Emily Cady wrote about such symptoms. She called it "chemicalization".

When we set an intention everything unlike that intention comes up to be healed. That is why things may seem to get worse before they get better. In years past, silversmiths would heat silver over a very hot fire in order to purify it and make sure that it was 100% silver. When the fire reached a certain temperature, everything that was not silver would rise to the top. It could, then, be skimmed off until only pure silver remained. A similar process happens when changes come into your life. Everything unlike those changes comes up to be "skimmed off". It comes up to be healed.

The longer you have held onto negative, limiting beliefs and habits the more likely symptoms will result. Symptoms can also result when you resist change. Emily Cady likens it to adding baking soda to vinegar; it bubbles up and causes a bit of a mess. If given enough time the mixture will settle down into a more neutral substance. It is the same when we set about to change an old paradigm. There may be a mess in the beginning but it will eventually settle down.

You may have physical symptoms such as headaches, nausea, body aches, flu-like symptoms, etc. You may experience memory lapses, confusion, mental fatigue or physical lethargy. There may be the inability to give your attention to things that used to interest you. Old habits and unwanted conditions that you thought were gone forever may briefly resurface. Old issues may come up that you thought that you had dealt with once and for all. As best you can, handle whatever that comes up and know that it is only temporary. You may want to enlist the help of a trusted friend, counselor or minister.

I am letting you know these things, not to place suggestions in your mind but to let you know that it is not unusual for these symptoms to appear. Your anxiety level is likely to be less if you know, in advance, about these possibilities. These symptoms are likely to disappear rather quickly.

If you are moving toward financial freedom, don't be surprised if your money situation seems to get worse before it gets better. If you are moving toward healing, don't be surprised if, for a short time, you feel worse. Remember, like the purification of silver, these things have come up to be "skimmed off". Keep working toward the goal that you have set for yourself. Persistence pays! Things will level off and wonderful, almost magical things will begin to happen! Don't allow temporary discouragement to reroute you from your intended goal.

When you get past the initial learning curve of the changes, so much energy is freed up that it seems like a miracle! This newly freed up energy will make the road ahead clearer and easier to navigate. This energy will propel you toward your heart's desire. Celebrate this milestone! Open yourself fully and completely to your good! **Your dream life awaits you!**

CONCLUSION

How Much Do You Want It?

When you showed up on this planet, greatness was born! You were created in the image and after the likeness of God Almighty, Creator of All! God endowed you with gifts that are uniquely yours and are meant to be shared with the world! You are a bright and shining star and your light is meant to help illuminate the world!

The heart's desires that are within you were placed there by The God of All Creation! In the same "package" with your heart's desires came everything that you will ever need to bring them to fruition! You either already have every tool and opportunity or they will show up as you need them. God is love and would not place within you a deep longing for your heart's desire and then say to you, "Too bad you don't have what it takes!" Of course not! You have what it takes and more!

You are the determining factor in creating your heart's desires. Only you hold the power to bring your dream into manifestation. It is God's good pleasure to give you the kingdom but God will not force it upon you. God has given you everything that is needed to create the dream that lives in your heart. But, you have to step up, do your part and claim it! No one can do for you that which you must do for yourself. *"You can't hire another person to do your push-ups."* Jim Rohn There are some things you must do for yourself.

God's part is done. Your heart's desire is already here in Spirit. You need only follow your guidance and step out in faith to receive it. The life of your dreams is ready to burst forth!

Don't limit yourself to what you or anyone else thinks is possible. Don't allow circumstances to dictate your future! Don't allow your old paradigm to talk you out of your dream simply because it has never been done. Spirit has been waiting for you to step up so that you could do the "impossible".

Are you willing to do whatever it takes to bring your heart's desire into reality? Effort will probably be required but not struggle. The responsibility of your dream lies with you. The "ball is in your court". The determining factor is, "How much do you want it?" Are you willing to go the extra mile when necessary? Are you willing to wait during the "incubation period"? Are you willing to stay the course until you reach your dream life?

You can have what you want in life. Will you reach a sustained point where everything in your life seems perfect, all of the time? Maybe not; life comes with challenges and opportunities for growth. You do have the capability of living your dream life, knowing that you are in your right and perfect place, doing what you are called to do. In short, it is very possible to build a life you love! **If I can do it, you can do it!**

The Universe leans in to support you!

This is your life!

Your time is now!

Be all that you came here to be!

Here's to

LIVING FULL-TILT!

To the Skeptic

If you are still skeptical about all or part of this book, I have this to say to you,

What if these principles and exercises really do work and you miss it? What if you let your skepticism stand in the way of you living the life of your dreams? Would you really want to think that you passed up a chance to move into a level of living that affords you opportunities that, up to this point, you barely would allow yourself to think about? Are you attached to your skepticism so strongly that you would take a chance on missing out? Do you have fear to such a degree that you would miss out on the life of your dreams? Is it worth it? If this seems like I am issuing a challenge; it is because I am. I tend to be a skeptic, as well, so I know some of the things that you are probably thinking. You may be thinking:

- Much of this seems too easy.
- I've tried some of these things in the past.
- If it really works why isn't everyone living their dream life?
- What will my friends think?
- Who does she think she is?

- I am too old, young, smart, dumb, tired, etc.
- Or, anything which helps you to *argue for your limitations.*

Here is what I have found in my life: When I get tired enough of having what I don't want, I will do whatever it takes to have what I do want.

Why not give the principles and exercises a six month try? If you keep breathing for the next six months you will create a life. Why not take a chance on living the life of your dreams?

My Story

I believe that I was born to do this work. I believe that I chose my family of origin, before I came into this life experience, so that I could experience poverty of all kinds (physical, emotional and spiritual) and know what it is like. Because of my beginnings, I can relate to those having similar challenges. There is a marked difference in reading about or viewing poverty than the experience of living in poverty. I know what it is like to live far below the poverty line. I know what it is like to be hungry with no food to eat. Because I know what it is like to live in poverty, I can talk about it and write about it in a way that I could not otherwise. My early life taught me that I wanted to live a better way and yet there was nothing in my young life that taught me how to do that. I believe that my parents did the very best that they knew how to do. They could not teach me a way of life that they did not know. They could not treat me in a way that they had not experienced. There is no one to blame even if I wanted to; which I do not. I only knew that I did not want to live my life in poverty. It continues to be a lifelong experience to learn how to live a better way.

I was born into a very poor family, the eldest of three children. Until I was about ten years old, my parents, my two siblings and I lived in a two-room house. There were two rooms for 5 people. Each of the two rooms was about 12' by 12'. The house had a front door a back door and 4 windows. There was no electricity, no running water and no indoor plumbing. That means that there were no electric lights, no refrigerator, or anything else that required electricity. There was a small propane stove for cooking. We had an outdoor toilet at the end of a path behind our house. There was a kitchen sink but the water was hauled in from a hand pump outside the back door. The pump had to be primed each time before it would give water. At sundown my mom would light our one kerosene lamp if we had kerosene for it. Much of the time we would just go to bed when it got dark. I remember not having enough to eat sometimes and feeling sad about the way we lived. When I went to the homes of other people and saw how they lived, I wondered why we did not have electric lights, water in our kitchen and a bathroom inside our house like they had. When I started to school I felt very embarrassed and ashamed about the way we lived. I remember that sometimes we did not have propane for our heater in the winter so we wrapped ourselves in homemade quilts to stay warm. Sometimes I didn't have enough clothing so I would hand wash things at night. Some of my most embarrassing times were when my classmates would call attention to the fact that I wore the same few pieces of clothing over and over. Most of the time there was not enough money to buy school supplies to do my school work, so, "borrowing" supplies from my classmates was almost a daily practice. I felt ashamed having to do it but it was the only way to do my school work. I put the word "borrowing" in quotation marks because I very rarely had anything to give back to them so they were actually giving school supplies to me. Sometimes their parents would tell them not to give me anything more. I didn't ask my friends to come to my house after school or on weekends because then they would see how we lived. In the second grade, one of my friends pressured me and I was too shy to say no so I let her get off the bus with me after school one day. All day at school I kept hoping that the whole thing would not be too unbearable or that she would change her mind and go home instead. It turned out to be a very embarrassing afternoon and a defining moment in my life. I vowed two things; I would never again allow my friends to come home with me and I also vowed that when I got to be an adult I would not live this way.

When I was about ten, my parents had a shell of a house built. Along with friends and family, they put up the walls, finished the painting, plumbing, woodwork and the rest of the interior themselves. The house had three bedrooms, a living room, a kitchen and, best of all; it had running water, a bathroom and electricity. I finally got to live in a house similar to my friends. I felt rich! It was to be a short lived feeling. Sometime after we moved into the new house our car was repossessed. I made up a story to tell my friends in an effort to avoid embarrassment about not having a car. In a small town people know almost everything about each other and my friends soon knew the truth; we had no money to make the car payments. During the period of living in the larger house there were many times that my parents feared that they would lose the house and property because they could not pay the house note. Often our electricity was turned off because of non-payment. Sometimes there was not enough money to buy propane in the winter months, so again, we had no heat. Still at times we did not have enough food, clothing and other necessities. My parents separated several times during my childhood and eventually divorced when I was about fourteen. Even in the new house, that would have seemed to be better, I still did not invite my friends over because I never knew what to expect when I got home. I did not want to risk the embarrassment.

My dad was an alcoholic and, to my knowledge, never got sober until he died at 64. Looking back, I see how his alcoholism played a big part in our lack of money. Many things went on in our home that fit the classic description of an alcoholic household. My sense of self-worth was very low as a result of my home environment. The dysfunction grew worse as the years went by. Before my parents divorced, my mom would have periods of days, weeks and months that she would stay in bed. To my knowledge, she did not have a physical illness. She would be in bed when I left for school and in bed when I came home. Being the eldest child, it was up to me to get my sister and brother off to school in the mornings and see that they had something to eat in the evenings. If Mom did not wake us up and I did not wake up in time, we would miss the bus and have to stay home from school. My grades suffered greatly as a result. In my young mind I interpreted the poor grades to mean that I was not smart. I did not connect my difficult home life and my absenteeism with my grades. School, in general, was very hard for me. Imagine my surprise when, as an adult, I took an IQ test and found that my ability to learn is above average. I am including this piece of information in order to point out that messages received in childhood can be false and yet quite damaging. Had I not taken the IQ test I would never have known that my early grades were not a true reflection of my abilities.

I got my driver's license at fourteen years of age and sometimes would take my siblings to after school activities when a car was available to me. I also shopped for food at a locally owned store where my parents had a credit agreement. Sometimes, if my parents had not paid on their bill in a long time, the store owners would only let me get a small amount and sometimes they would not let me have anything until a payment was made. As in most alcoholic households, I learned early not to talk about certain things that happened at home. There are many more stories that are much more difficult than the ones I have written but it would serve no good purpose to tell them here. My reason for telling these few stories is so that you would get an overview of my beginnings.

From the age of about five, I knew that this was not the way that I wanted to live. There was a knowing within me that I could live a better life than the one that I was experiencing and yet there was nothing in my world that told me how to do that. There was a time when I blamed my parents for the shame that I felt about the way that we lived. I have made peace with my parents and I know that they did the best that they knew how to do based on the experience of their own lives. I know that is true because I gave my own children the best that I had to give at the time that I raised them and I know that I fell short in many ways.

I have come to believe that I made a soul agreement to have the parents that I had and to live the way that I lived. It has helped me to have compassion for people going through similar life situations. It has given me a heart to teach the Truth Principles governing prosperity and to help others know that they absolutely can live the life of their dreams.

I continue to learn and grow as I teach. I definitely do not do everything perfectly. I am still learning. It is a part of my mission in life to help you know that you have choices. No matter how your life began, no matter how many mistakes you have made along the way, living the life of your dreams is still possible! There have been times that I, too, have thought that life was an endless series of hopeless conditions and circumstances. I felt that life had thrown these circumstances at me and it was up to me to make the best of them and keep putting one foot in front of another. I have not always known that I had choices. I have not always known that I am a co-creator with God for my life. I continue to learn this Truth at a deeper level.

Having lived like I did as a child, it is no wonder that I grew up to re-enact many of those situations in my adult life. I lived the paradigm that I knew. When I was 17, I married a man who was an alcoholic/drug addict. He was physically, verbally and emotionally abusive. He hit me on many occasions and threatened to kill me if I told anyone. I lived in a state of constant terror the entire time that we were married. I was living in abuse similar to what I had as a child. I did not know any better. I left him for the last time when, during a beating, it suddenly dawned on me that our nine month old baby was next. I knew that he would, eventually, abuse him verbally and beat him the same as he had done to me. At that point I had a deep inner knowing that I would do whatever it took to get us out of that situation. Over the next few years, my son and I lived with various relatives for protection.

I tell this story, not to evoke sympathy, but to help you to know some of my life experiences. After much counseling and a lifetime of experience, I now know that, as adults, we set up some of the same circumstances from our childhood so that we can heal them within ourselves. Unconsciously, I kept setting up the same set of abusive, limiting and impoverished circumstances not knowing how to correct them. Over time, I have made healthier and healthier choices.

I made a decision not to include many of my life stories and I have purposely left out details because I have no need for revenge or to hurt other people who were involved in my life.

With the help of a wonderful therapist, The Twelve Step Program and a magnificent spiritual teacher in the form of a Unity minister, I began to learn how to heal the very deep wounds and start to make some different life choices. I am now married to a kind and loving man, I have robust health, and I have work that I lose myself in because it is not really work to me. I have freedom to move toward being all that I came here to be and am still learning how to manifest the resources to do all of the things that I really want to do. I am living a life based in joy that does not depend upon other people or outer circumstances. Much of the time, I feel the innate joy that pours forth from within. Today I live the life that I used to only dream about. It all happened because of my life experiences and learning how to live in cooperation with Spiritual Principles. Just as I learned (and am learning) to cooperate with these Spiritual Principles, you can too. No matter where you are in life, no matter what choices you have made in the past, no matter how far down you may find yourself, there is a way up and out. You have the power to live the life of your dreams!

If I can do it, you can do it!

I bless you on your way!

Suggested Reading

Bijan, **Absolutely Effortless Prosperity**

Claude M. Bristol, **The Magic of Believing**

Les Brown, **Live Your Dreams**

Eric Butterworth, **Spiritual Economics**

Emily Cady, **Lessons in Truth**

Jack Canfield, **The Success Principles**

Deepak Chopra, **Seven Spiritual Laws of Success**

Stephen Covey, **Seven Habits of Highly Effective People**

Wayne Dyer, **The Power of Intention**

Charles Fillmore, **Prosperity**

Mark Fisher, **How to Think Like A Millionaire**

Mark Fisher, **The Instant Millionaire**

Edwene Gaines, **The Four Spiritual Laws of Prosperity**

Shakti Gawain, **Creative Visualization**

Louise Hay, **You Can Heal Your Life**

Phil Laut, **Money Is My Friend**

Mary Katherine McDougall, **What Treasure Mapping Can Do for You** (booklet)

L. E. Meyer, **As You Tithe So You Prosper** (booklet)

Mary Morrissey, **Building Your Field of Dreams**

Mary Morrissey, **No Less Than Greatness**

Jeffery Moses, **Oneness**

Maria Nemeth, **The Energy of Money**

Catherine Ponder, **The Dynamic Laws of Prosperity**

Catherine Ponder, **Open Your Mind to Receive**

John Randolph Price, **The Abundance Book**

Jim Rosemergy, **Even Mystics Have Bills to Pay**

Jon Speller, **Seed Money in Action** (booklet)

Stuart Wilde, **The Secret of Money is Having Some**

Stuart Wilde, **Life Was Never Meant to Be a Struggle**

Coleen Zuck, Patricia Tinney, Laura Harvey, **Daily Word for Prosperity**

85684718R00143

Made in the USA
Lexington, KY
03 April 2018